My Journey in tl

Jesus Christ

Spiritual Healing Authoress

Adriana Brunga

Dedicatory

I am filled with immense gratitude and appreciation towards the Holy Spirit for guiding me in the creation of this extraordinary book. With Divine inspiration, I have delved deeply into the teachings of Jesus Christ, and it is my utmost desire to convey my thoughts and insights to readers, spreading a powerful message of love and salvation.

With the deepest gratitude, this message serves as a heartfelt tribute to our dear departed sons Jose and Diego Pineda. It serves as a poignant reminder of the eternal love and unbreakable bond the author cherishes for them. Furthermore, it expresses sincere appreciation towards our family for their unwavering fortitude and assistance during this arduous time. Additionally, special acknowledgment is extended to my husband, Bruno Brunga, for his unwavering support and strength.

Continually, I cannot emphasize enough the significance of Amazon Pro's contributions to this amazing book. Their unwavering commitment, special dedication, and exceptional skills have undoubtedly played a pivotal role in its success. It is with immense gratitude and appreciation that I thank Amazon Pro for their tireless efforts in bringing this project to fruition. Without their professionalism and expertise, this exemplary would not have achieved the same level of excellence. Their immense contributions and unwavering support will always be remembered and treasured.

Preface

This book is based on a real-life story that will touch your heart and miraculously change the way you see God. - This book will help you realize that only God can give you the strength and courage you need to get through the most difficult storm. -

It all started like this; This is the story of a three-year-old girl who created her own shelter house in her mind. Who found peace, love, joy, faith, and a wonderful God in the Bible. This little girl is now forty-six years old, but due to a post-traumatic event, she ended up with a mysterious mental illness called "Conversion Disorder", (a post-traumatic stress disorder).

This mysterious mental illness causes her brain to make involuntary mindless movements in her mind, creating an automated mental regression; making her talk and act like a three-year-old girl. - When this happens, she automatically goes to her perfect hiding place inside an imaginary empty room, allowing her spirit to feel protected and loved by God. -

After returning from a coma and death, she found the most interesting complement and purpose in life. - Jesus Christ! Jesus Christ Blessed her directly from Heaven; and sent her back with a mission to fulfill. -

Today, she has a story to tell, and she is happy to share this lovely story with all of you. - This story is not just a common story; This is a mysterious real-life event that can happen to anyone in this life. - God has chosen her for a reason, and only He knows the end of her story. -

Spiritual author,

My Journey in the Afterlife with Jesus Christ

Introduction

Today, I want to share my life story with you. - After reading this story, it is quite possible that the way you think about God will change. - The main concepts of this story are salvation and God's permissive will.

Why salvation? - The Bible says,

9 because if you acknowledge and confess with your mouth that Jesus is Lord [recognizing His power, authority, and majesty as God], and believe in your heart that God raised Him from the dead, you will be saved. (Romans 10:9) AMB

Salvation frees us from a possible spiritual prison in which we may be; it is the only way out of it; a prison to which we arrive because of our sins, and only Jesus Christ can free us.

For thirty-two years, I lived my life thinking that everyone was against me, not realizing that the one who was against me was myself. - I was a very unhappy person. I constantly isolated myself from everyone and acted irrationally on many occasions; provoking arguments with the people around me and who loved me. - I blamed my mother for many years, for not divorcing my dad in time, but she never knew.

It was extremely difficult for me to understand why she did not divorce my dad back then, but I guess God works in mysterious ways. - Today, I clearly see the reason, and the purpose of my life in the way God created me. - He allowed me to go through difficult valleys in life, letting me see how He answered my prayers. -

“When you do not forgive others, it is like drinking poison, expecting the other person to die. - Without realizing that the one who is dying is you.” How can we expect God to forgive us if we do not forgive others? -

2 with all humility [forsaking self-righteousness], and gentleness [maintaining self-control], with patience, bearing with one another [a]in [unselfish] love. - (Ephesians 4:2) AMB

It is particularly important to understand that if we forgive others, we can receive Heavenly forgiveness from our Father, God, in Heaven. Without His forgiveness, we cannot free ourselves from the spiritual prison in which we may be captive.

After all these years, I finally understand the power of God's Word and the true meaning of His message. - I want to share with you, how I lived my life before in my childhood, and a little bit of my mature life; I was full of resentment, and forgiveness from God, I had bitterness in my heart, sadness, and a lot of fear, but especially I was full of terror in my soul. -

I want to show you, through my thoughts and occurrences, how God one day changed my destiny forever, just like that! - We often like to plan for our future, our career paths, and even our children's future and destiny. However, we forget the primary author of our lives, God. -

Why is it so important to count on God in every decision we make? - The answer might be because He is God. He is the Creator of Heaven, the Creator of the universe, and the earth and everything in it, including us, you, and me. Or the answer could also be because Jesus Christ is the author and finisher of our lives.

13 "I am the Alpha and the Omega, the First and the Last, the Beginning and the End [the Eternal One]." -Revelation 22:13 AMB

Jesus Christ is the Almighty, and He has a purpose for our lives. - He is the only one who knows what is best for us because He created us all for a purpose. - I am totally convinced that apart from God, we can do nothing. - That means that if we do not count on Him in every area of our lives, He will leave us alone, and we won't be able to experience His favor. - Then, our lives became complicated and harder to live. - However, when we have the favor of Jesus Christ, all doors open automatically. -

My Journey in the Afterlife with Jesus Christ, is based on a real-life story. - For the most part, we may think that life is hard to live and that after we die, we can start a new life in paradise. But this is not the case. However, while living in this world, we may think that we are living a passing life, without recognizing the real purpose that allows us to enjoy the full path in our life of salvation that God has prepared for us. -

I want to explain to you that eternal life really begins when we are born again in Christ. Jesus Christ died for us to pay for our sins, to give us salvation, and free us from sin! The Bible says:

9 because if you acknowledge and confess with your mouth that Jesus is Lord [recognizing His power, authority, and majesty as God], and believe in your heart that God raised Him from the dead, you will be saved. -(Romans 10:9) AMB

The more you read the Bible, the more freedom you will have, and the truth will set you free. When I was in a coma for five days, I did not know much about God. - After meeting Jesus Christ face to face, my life changed, completely and forever. -

The reason I titled this book My Journey in the Afterlife with Jesus Christ is because I lived spiritual death for thirty-two years until Jesus Christ came to my rescue and saved my life eternally. - In addition, I experienced physical death and came back to life to fully understand the real value and purpose of my existence. - Wow! - Two different deaths in one body; That is an amazing thing! -

I am ready to open my heart to tell you part of the story of my life and show you who Jesus Christ is. - My story may not be like yours, but ultimately, we all suffer spiritual death (separated from God) in some way. - Are you ready? - Let's go!

Table of Contents

Part Number One
Scene One: The Birth of Resilience: How Every Comeback Started with a Setback

Chapter 1

The Chronicle of my Childhood: A Memoir

What is Spiritual Death?

Spiritual death is when someone is physically alive, but spiritually dead. Technically, the Light of the Lord, the true living God, has not yet reached within you. All of us are born spiritually dead, that is, separated from God. - The Lord said to Adam:

And the Lord God commanded the man, saying,

**"You may freely (unconditionally) eat [the fruit] from every tree of the garden; 17 but [only] from the tree of the knowledge (recognition) of good and evil you shall not eat, otherwise on the day that you eat from it, you shall most certainly [a]die [because of your disobedience]."*

(Genesis 2:16–17) AMB

**(the tree of conscious understanding, between good and evil or a full and alert awareness of the recognition of sin in our lives).*

Now, Mankind is separated from God by nature. - Jesus said:

"I assure you and most solemnly say to you, the person who hears My word [the one who heeds My message], and believes and trusts in Him who sent Me, has (possesses now) eternal life [that is, eternal life actually begins—the believer is transformed], and does not come into judgment and condemnation, but has passed [over] from death into life. - (John 5:24) AMB

Although my father and my mother have abandoned me, Yet the Lord will take me up [adopt me as His child]. - (Psalm 27:10) AMB

I remember one morning when I was sitting in front of a window, when I was just a child; my heart was filled with fear, terror, and condemnation. - My dad was a genuinely generous and nice person, but when he drank alcohol, he would automatically get mad at my mom for no reason. - In Colombia, South America, back in the 70s, when women got married, they did not have the right to express themselves. They literally had no rights. -My mom was a very patient being who worked very hard for all of us. - She worked cleaning houses for years. That way, she was able to support us financially. -

For thirteen years, I had to watch the way my dad treated my mom. I had to watch how, after getting drunk, my dad would turn into someone else, depositing his anger on my mom for no reason. - My brother Carlos, and I had to hide many times in a safe place. - For many years I created in my mind a secret and safe place to stay and never escape from there. All I had in mind was this Bible verse:

You are my hiding place; You, Lord, protect me from trouble; You surround me with songs and shouts of deliverance. - (Psalm 32:7) AMB

I remember one day, my dad was giving us dinner, but my brother and I did not want to eat at that time. - My dad got so angry that he forced us to eat, making us vomit and eat off the floor. -

I describe fear as the scariest feeling a person can have. - This makes you feel like a person you cannot define, paralyzing your emotions and feelings; paralyzing their movements by responding to the appropriate actions in life, producing terror, insecurity, and trauma in your mind. - My mother had to work hard to support us financially, and sometimes, she did not have time to talk to us or understand our feelings.

- All she used to say was, "This storm shall pass. This is not going to last forever." -

Once, when my mom came home from work around six o'clock at night, my dad showed up at the house very drunk. - She was in the kitchen, making us dinner. - She had a pan of hot oil on the stove. - My dad started hitting her for no reason. - She cried and asked for help. - She did not know what to do, but she got angry and threw the hot oil on dad's chest, making him more angry and violent. - I ran away from the house very scared and asked for help. "Someone calls the police, please!" I yelled. -

Meanwhile, my dad was constantly beating my mom, causing her to lose consciousness. - I saw this violence for thirteen years. - And I kept it in my heart. - This happened almost every day until I was thirteen. -

He will cover you and completely protect you with His pinions, and under His wings you will find refuge; His faithfulness is a shield and a wall. You will not be afraid of the terror of night, nor of the arrow that flies by day, nor of the pestilence that stalks in darkness, nor of the destruction (sudden death) that lays waste at noon. - (Psalm 91:4–6) AMB

My mom suffered constant physical pain, but I suffered spiritual and emotional agony. As I mentioned, I developed a condition called "Conversion Disorder," (a post-traumatic panic disorder). Every tear that my mom shed in her eyes, I kept inside my heart. - When you combine fear and terror together, it creates the most terrifying feeling a person can ever feel, with a sense of alert escape!

We must forgive, no matter what. -

'And forgive us our [a]debts, as we have forgiven our debtors [letting go of both the wrong and resentment]. 13 'And do not [b]lead us into temptation but deliver us from [c]evil. [d] [For Yours is the kingdom and the power and the glory forever. Amen.]' 14 For if you forgive [e]others their trespasses [their reckless and willful sins], your heavenly Father will also forgive you. 15 But if you do not forgive others [nurturing your hurt and anger with the result that it interferes with your relationship with God], then your Father will not forgive your trespasses. (See Matthew 6:12–15.) AMB

As life went on, I realized how much God loved me. - As much as we had to deal with harmful experiences, God always protected me and helped me through difficult adversities in life.

- He gave me a solid comfort of peace, strength, wisdom, and serenity to understand what I could not change at that moment. -

Only God could understand the agony I felt in the depths of my soul, every time my dad hit my mom. It was as if an arrow pierced my heart; leaving a void full of anguish inside me. I did not know how many angels I had around me until I experienced domestic violence for thirteen years.

- We all have a destiny; We all have a purpose in life. - No matter how many rocks we have in front of us, we must move them aside and keep walking in faith. - God always makes sure to redirect our steps to where He wants us to be. - I grew up thinking more like an adult than a child. At the age of eight, I could do the housework, and cook, very well. - I had to live my life incredibly fast and not enjoy my childhood very much. -

“For God so [greatly] loved and dearly prized the world, that He [even] gave His [One and] [a]only begotten Son, so that whoever believes and trusts in Him [as Savior] shall not perish but have eternal life. - (John 3:16) AMB

There was also something very remarkable about my dad that set him apart from other people and made him unique. - His kindness and generosity attracted many people around him when he was not drunk. - My dad tried to act rationally, but he died, not knowing about the truth of Jesus Christ. He did not have enough time to learn about his bad drinking behavior, and he never realized how talented he was. -

It was then that I deeply understood the despair that he had within his heart. -Today, I understand his circumstances and the reasons why he could not be himself. - His cheerful outlook, kindness, and generosity helped me find my identity as a special being; The person I am today. - My mom always told us: only learn the good from people. -

While all these things were happening, God was mysteriously beginning to work in my life, giving me a great insight into my mind. - I never knew why I was so kind, generous, loving, and, most of all, a sweet person. - A lot of people took advantage of me for that. Many times, I asked myself: Why am I doing this? - I understood, later in life, the meaning of my behavior. - God not only had a dream inside my heart, but He gave a special calling on my life.

On the morning of November 1, 1989, that day, the rain was falling, and the day was very opaque, my dad disappeared. Yes, he was kidnapped for several days; I felt an urgent need to find him. - Around six in the morning, his friend George arrived at the house, looking for him. - As I was on my way to school with my brother, George asked me, "Is your dad in the house?" - I replied, "Yes, it is." - Two minutes later, my dad yelled at me, "Why did you tell him I was here?" - He was screaming senselessly through the window; I did not know why he told me that. But, five days later, my dad's body was found in a mass grave. I asked my mom if she would let me identify my dad's corpse. - And she allowed me to do it, only because, at the time, she was seven months pregnant with my sister Laura. -

I did not want her to see my dad like that. - I went to different morgues, trying to find my dad, but I could not find him. - Fortunately, five days later, my mom received a phone call from my aunt Susan, who worked at the police station. - She confirmed the appearance of my dad's corpse. - My dad's death was incredibly sad for many people, but it was devastating and traumatic for me. -

We discovered that he had been tortured, hanged, and buried. I could see all this in the spirit on the day of his death as a vision in my mind; I do not know why. - The day he disappeared; I felt something strange inside me. - For thirty-two years, I felt guilty and condemned for my dad's death. I was convinced that he had been murdered because I had told my dad's friend that he was in the house. - I held that guilt for thirty-two years in my heart, thinking that his death was a simple thing to understand. - Unfortunately, this left me with remarkable, unforgettable, and irreversible memories. -

I always asked God to allow me to see my dad again one day so I could ask him for forgiveness. - My mom ended up raising three children on her own. - Months later, she decided to move to The United States because Pablo Escobar's people, who had killed my dad, were looking for us to kill us, too. - We did not understand why. - We had to live away from my mom for two years. - That moment was nerve-wracking for the three of us. - During this time, my aunt and grandmother took care of us. -

Unfortunately, they were not able to stay long with us because they moved to another town about an hour away from us. - They took my sister Laura, who was only a few months old, and left my brother, and I alone in our own house in Envigado. - We had to find a way to survive. Day by day, we face many challenges. Sometimes, we did not have food to eat. -

I thank the Lord for putting two wonderful women on our path who helped us a lot: my aunt Susan, who allowed me to work in her house as a cleaner and take care of my cousins to earn some money, and Chila, my neighbor, who fed me at least once a day. - She was the first person to teach me about Jesus Christ. -

"I will not leave you as orphans [comfortless, bereaved, and helpless]; I will come [back] to you. (John 14:18) AMB

Two years passed, and my mother brought us to this Blessed land. - God never left us alone, as He promised. - He did not abandon us. -

Instead, He put the right people in our path to help us. When I arrived in The United States, I had big dreams in mind. I always wanted to be someone special to people. - Years later, I fell in love and started a new life with Milton Pineda. - I deeply thank him for all the love and care he gave me for twenty-two years. Today, we have three wonderful adult children: Jose, Sarah, and Diego. - They are my life and the reason for my existence. - God works in an enigmatic way. - He knows the purpose of our lives from the moment He created us. -

He will not stop until He completes the full purpose of His will in our lives. - For many years, my heart was filled with emptiness, discouragement, sadness, hopelessness, resentment, hatred, and unworthiness. - I walked through life with dry bones inside me; My heart was carrying negative emotions, making me feel bad and tired. - I walked through life with extremely low self-esteem, without hope and without love. In fact, I always thought that no one loved me at all. The only thing I had was the little house I had drawn in my mind when I was a child; This little house was my safe place to hide. - I discovered that I was just a little girl trapped in this little glass house, with a Bible protecting my soul and my heart that was inside me in my spirit.

You are my hiding place; You, Lord, protect me from trouble; You surround me with songs and shouts of deliverance. - (Psalm 32:7) AMB

At a certain point in my life, I realized that I had been stillborn, alive. - I was a human being, walking into the darkness of the world. - My heart was captured in my own prison of terror, fear, and loneliness within me for years. - Today, I understand that God never left me alone. - He was my refuge during times of adversity. - He protected me with His own wings to comfort me, and He put a high calling on my heart, long before I was born. - He knew that I had to go through all these circumstances, to make me stronger, and braver, to understand the difficulties of life. - Circumstances happen for a reason, and sometimes, it is hard to understand and accept them. -

Why? - Because as you go through life, and God begins to reveal to you the meaning of your purpose, that is when life begins to take its proper place. - Today, I thank God for all the bad experiences I had, because, thanks to that, I am who I am in Christ. - For years, I lived my life full of sadness; I allowed the spirit of darkness (resentment, loneliness, or any negative emotion) to pollute my heart, even my physical body. - My emotions, feelings, thoughts, and will (soul) were corrupted early in the younger years of my life. -

I was able to make the most crucial decision a person can make in their early life. -My mom asked me, when I was eight years old, "Which path in life do you want to take, the good or the bad?" - Trust me; I did not hesitate to choose the good one, but some people choose the wrong one, because of the resentment they have in their hearts. - They cannot control their emotions, or feelings, simply because it is so difficult to do so, without Jesus Christ in their hearts. -

How many people have chosen to act badly against other people? - Many people think that someone has something to repay them, but in reality, no one can repay you for the spiritual pain you endured in life. - No one can give you what they do not owe you. No one needs to live through the traumas or bad experiences you went through. - Everyone has their own experiences and responsibilities. - Only God, Jesus Christ, the true living God, can give you the spiritual restoration you lack because before we were human beings, we were spirits. -

To produce spiritual fuel, we must forgive those who hurt us and forgive ourselves for being part of the circumstances. - That way, our Heavenly Father, God, in Heaven, can forgive us and give us the spiritual renewal we need. - If you are going through a difficult spiritual pain today, I counsel you to surrender yourself to the Spirit of the Lord, Jesus Christ, the only living and true God, and confess to Him what you feel. - Ask Him to forgive you. - At the same time, you must forgive those who have hurt you, and you will receive full Blessings from Heaven and walk in life with victory! - This requires a humble heart that is ready to begin a new chapter in life. -

Forgiveness is not a Feeling- It is a decision we make

- Are you tired of living the life you have?

- Do you feel like you are going up and down the same mountain, repeatedly, and it seems like you are going nowhere?

-Have you felt resentment against someone for years, and your heart doesn't seem to feel any better? Have your thoughts been stuck in the same place for years?

-Do you feel like you have been trapped in a spiritual prison all your life?

It is time to make the most crucial decision you will ever make in your life: surrender to the Lord and forgive. - It is time to start a new chapter in your life. - Trust me; -You won't regret it. - You deserve it! - Forgiveness is not a feeling. - It is a decision you make. -Remember that!

Let us pray together,

Heavenly Father, I love You. Thank You for always being there for me. Thank You for not leaving me unprotected during adversity. Thank You for allowing me to be a part of the circumstances that only made me stronger and braver. - Lord Jesus, help me to continue in life. - Help me to forgive those I love most. - Remove from me any resentment planted in my heart. - Please forgive me for being a victim of these circumstances. - Thank You for giving me the courage, wisdom, and understanding in times of need. - Thank You for Your promises that only made me stronger and more faithful to You. - In the name of Jesus Almighty, I pray. - Amen.

Chapter 2

The Transforming Power of Jesus Christ: How He Turned my Accident into a Blessing

Jesus answered, "I assure you and most solemnly say to you, unless one is born of water and the Spirit, he cannot [ever] enter the kingdom of God. 6 That which is born of the flesh is flesh [the physical is merely physical], and that which is born of the Spirit is spirit. 7 Do not be surprised that I have told you, 'You must be born again [reborn from above—spiritually transformed, renewed, sanctified].' 8 The wind blows where it wishes, and you hear its sound, but you do not know where it is coming from and where it is going; so, it is with everyone who is born of the Spirit."

— (John 3:5-8) AMB

Once more Jesus addressed the crowd. He said, "[a]I am the Light of the world. He who follows Me will not walk in the darkness but will have the Light of life."

— (John 8:12) AMB

Scripture says we need to die (spiritually) to be born again and become a new creature in Christ. - What does it really mean? - It means that at certain times in our lives, we need to surrender to God, denying ourselves to receive the Lord into our hearts. This means truly admitting that without God, we can do nothing. It is the recognition of the will given by God.

In addition, it is surrendering your will to the Lord, so that God will take control of your life.

Then Jesus said to His disciples,

"If anyone wishes to follow Me [as My disciple], he must deny himself [set aside selfish interests], and take up his cross [expressing a willingness to endure whatever may come] and follow Me [believing in Me, conforming to My example in living and, if need be, suffering or perhaps dying because of faith in Me]. 25 For whoever wishes to save his life [in this world] will [eventually] lose it [through death], but whoever loses his life [in this world] for My sake will find it [that is, life with Me for all eternity]. 26 For what will it profit a man if he gains the whole world [wealth, fame, success], but forfeits his soul? Or what will a man give in exchange for his soul? (See Matthew 16:24–26)

I am about to share with you a real testimony, which relates how I lost my life physically and spiritually. At the same time, I became a new Christian person without expecting it.

It was a cold morning in October 2009, I ended up in a coma in a hospital bed. I was in the hands of God and the Doctors. - However, I never knew what the Lord had in store for me. Prior to that event, I was an extremely healthy person and ran my own import/export agency for five years. - I had an accident that changed my life forever. - It all started like this.

I went to the kitchen, looking for a glass of water, and slipped on a piece of ice that was on the floor. - I do not know how the ice cube ended up on the ground, but it happened. I did not feel any pain when I fell in an instant, but two months later, I started to feel pain in my lower spine. - After a while, the pain in my lower spine increased tremendously, and a month later, I ended up in the operating room with surgery on my lower spine. - Dr. Lehman, who was my surgeon, was incredibly surprised that the L4 and L5 discs were extremely ruptured. - The Doctor had to remove two discs from my spinal cord. - The Doctor exclaimed, "I have never seen anything like it before!" -

The surgery was carried out, ending successfully. After the surgery, he told us, "Adriana may not have walked again", but I refused to end up like this. - Months later. My recovery faltered a lot. - I was taking more than forty pills a day because my brain, body, and mind were completely dysfunctional. - I could barely walk and endure the chronic pain caused by the accident.

Suddenly, my health declined dramatically. - One day, I woke up in a very bad state. - I called nine one-one, and an ambulance took me to the hospital; The paramedics rushed me to the emergency room. - I was knocked unconscious. - I was quickly transferred to another hospital for better help. - The Doctor told my husband (at the time), Milton, "She is in a coma, but her brain won't stop moving." - My brain was acting mysteriously. -

The Doctors were incredibly surprised at how my brain worked during that time. - That was the most shocking news Milton, and my family received. - I ended up in a coma for five days. - After the fifth day, I opened my eyes but did not recognize anyone at all; I had a brain reset in my mind. - My family cried in pain and despair, not understanding what was happening to me. - The Doctors sent me to another hospital so that I could recover better the next day. When I arrived at the other hospital, it was around six o'clock at night. - I could not speak, see, or even walk properly. - I was like a newborn baby because I had had a brain reset. -

I arrived at the hospital expecting the Doctors to help me recover. - However, something unexpected happened around seven o'clock at night. - I stood up, looked at the ceiling, and said, "Thank you, Lord. I will give you everything!" - Everyone in the waiting room was extremely amazed! - "This is a miracle. What is going on in this place?" - the patients exclaimed. - When I opened my eyes, the first thing I saw was Jesus Christ walking toward me.

When Jesus Christ first appeared, I saw a man walking toward me in a purple robe and a golden scarf, looking at me very determined and serious. - Everything went dark. - My eyes were opened only to see the Lord; Then I noticed that my spiritual eyes opened for the first time. - Everyone was speechless; they all wanted to hear my conversation with Jesus Christ, the true living God. I heard patients cry softly, saying, "This is a miracle!" - I was led by The Holy Spirit. My conversation went on and on for minutes. - Suddenly, when Jesus Christ came to me, I fainted on the ground. The nurses sat me in a wheelchair and then laid me lightly on my bed. I lost my life at that moment. The nurse checked me many times. -

I was cold; My hands and face turned purple, and my heart stopped beating. - She exclaimed, "We lost her! - She is dead!" The nurse injected me with an injection to see if I could come back to life. - They tried everything to bring me back to life, but nothing worked. I could see my body lying lifeless on the bed, hearing everything around me. My family cried heartbreakingly. - At that moment, my spirit left my body, and I could see everything around me. During that time, I was lost in the world. -

My spirit floated everywhere, and I ran, looking for a place to stay. - I cried out to the Lord, saying, "Jesus, help me! I do not want to die!" - Mysteriously, my soul sank into a shadowy hole. - The hole was very dark, as if you were traveling through a dark tunnel, but out of nowhere, I found myself going to a boiling and roasting lake. - The lake had a different mix of textures and shades: a combination of orange, red, brown, yellow, and black. - Many people were screaming, asking me for help. - I was going terribly fast, and I was afraid of dying. - I cried out to the Lord, saying, "Help me, Jesus!" - Jesus immediately stretched out His hand to me, rescuing me from the death of hell.

Jesus Christ lifted me up quickly. Because,

for "whoever calls on the name of the Lord [in prayer] will be saved." ... (Romans 10:13) AMB

I was traveling through a Light, white, luminous tunnel at more than a thousand miles an hour. - I immediately felt peace in my heart, a peace I had never felt before. It is difficult to explain; The place felt very quiet. - I could see the speed of the air as I traveled within the clouds; Everything was in slow motion. - At some point, we stopped. - I found myself floating in space; It was dark but very quiet. - I could see the difference between the dark hole; the white and luminous tunnel; and the darkness of space. - I immediately knew I was going to Heaven. Suddenly, very quickly, I went from space to Heaven. - The place was quiet, peaceful, beautiful, and joyful, surrounded by clouds and a Heavenly glow. -

My heart rejoiced with joy and peace. For a moment, I found myself floating in the sky, with no gravity, no noise, and no people around me. - I felt no physical or emotional pain. - I was young, beautiful, and healthy. - It was certainly a place I did not want to leave. - The Lord was there with me the whole time. -

I jumped and ran like a little kid. - Suddenly, my dad appeared. Yes, I had prayed to the Lord for twenty-four years to allow me to see my dad again and to be able to ask him for forgiveness one day, and He granted it. - I found my dad sitting at the entrance of Heaven with a sad face. - He gave me the biggest hug he had ever had and said, "I am so sorry, daughter, for all the things I have done to you. "I love you so much. - I am here to take care of you and protect you." I cried with a deep pain in my heart. - I could not believe what my eyes and heart felt at that moment. -

After a while, Jesus took my hand and asked, "What do you want me to do for you, daughter?" I did not respond at the time. - I was so happy in that place that I did not want to leave. - He asked me a second time, "What do you want me to do for you, daughter?" - I found myself confused, without any answer. Suddenly, I heard a lot of whispers near my right ear. It came with force from somewhere, but I did not know what it was.

Soon, I realized that they were prayers from people asking Jesus to bring me back to life. -After I cried and heard those prayers, I said, "Lord, I would like my life back." - Jesus replied, "Okay, daughter. - I will give you your life back. But I need you to do something for Me." What is it, Lord?" I Answered. - "Tell the world about Me," Jesus said. - I quickly replied, "Yes, Lord! I will." - I thought for a moment that talking about the Lord was not a big deal until I wrote this book. -

Then, Jesus touched my forehead quickly, and immediately, my spirit was traveling at what seemed like a thousand miles per hour. Meanwhile, my body lay lifeless on the bed, not knowing what was going to happen next. - I felt a strange energy inside me, but no one knew It was there. - Within seconds, my Spirit re-entered my body. I quickly jumped out of bed and knelt on the floor. - I thanked the Lord for my life and cried out to the nurses for help. - I said, "Jesus is here!" - I could not see at the time, but the Lord's love allowed me to speak. - The Doctors told me they could not believe what they were seeing. - People in the hospital were amazed and said, "This is a miracle of life. She is a miracle of life." - The nurses were afraid to touch me, but from a distance, I could hear their voices. -

My life was transformed from that moment on. My mind, soul, and spirit changed completely. In fact, I was another person in the same body. My dad disappeared from my life when I was eleven and never came back after he disappeared. I was so Blessed to see him again at the entrance of Heaven and give him the last hug I had dreamed of having for all those years. God touched my heart deeply. He transformed my life unexpectedly. I was in the hospital for better help and ended up being Blessed.

Months later, I was permanently disabled due to my lower spine injury, but that did not stop me from doing what I needed to do for my kids or myself. - From that moment on, my life changed drastically and completely. God's Will began to take place in my life. Today, I have new dreams, a new life, a new me, and a new beginning. I love my life. - I love Jesus Christ and this beautiful world He created. - I learned to appreciate the unimportant things in life more than ever before. - I am here to fulfill God's promise; the great purpose He has for me. I have a special calling from Him, a calling that has been alive in my heart from the first moment I met Jesus Christ of Nazareth. -

Therefore, humble yourselves under the mighty hand of God [set aside self-righteous pride], so that He may exalt you [to a place of honor in His service] at the appropriate time, (1 Peter 5:6) AMB

For the first time in my life, I felt alive! - Jesus Christ lives in me! - The Spirit of the Lord is in me! - Hallelujah! - When Jesus Christ appeared in my life, He gently touched my heart, restoring my soul, converting my spirit, and transforming me into a new creature. God is love, and He is merciful. - I understood why we need to die spiritually to receive God's true love and be born again. - When we are firstborn, we come with a veil covering our eyes that does not allow us to see the love of the Lord. - This is known as an original sin. - God says, because,

for "whoever calls on the name of the Lord [in prayer] will be saved." ... (Romans 10:13) AMB

We must confess with our mouth that Jesus is the Son of God to receive righteousness in Christ. - After that, I learned to live my life full of joy, love, and Blessings, just because I know who I am in Christ. - I became spiritual. - I clearly understood that God does not need our bodies. - He is here to rescue our souls and live in our spirits through the Holy Spirit.

I value this precious life more than ever. - I am a newborn again in Jesus Christ. - I was able to understand that everything that happened in my life was not so bad. - I can only say that everything I experienced happened for a reason, regardless of the circumstances I had. - This only prepared me to become a better person today, allowing me to give myself totally and completely to the Lord and recognize God's true love.

Therefore, humble yourselves under the mighty hand of God [set aside self-righteous pride], so that He may exalt you [to a place of honor in His service] at the appropriate time, (1 Peter 5:6) AMB

Even the pain I endured in my soul and body was digging something into me that carried a great presence of God in my life.

The Bible says.

What then shall we say to all these things? If God is for us, who can be [successful] against us? 32 He who did not spare [even] His own Son, but gave Him up for us all, how will He not also, along with Him, graciously give us all things? 33 Who will bring any charge against God's elect (His chosen ones)? It is God who justifies us [declaring us blameless and putting us in a right relationship with Himself]. 34 Who is the one who condemns us? Christ Jesus is the One who died [to pay our penalty], and more than that, who was raised [from the dead], and who is at the right hand of God interceding [with the Father] for us. 35 Who shall ever separate us from the love of [a]Christ? Will tribulation, distress, or persecution, or famine, or nakedness, or danger, or sword? 36 Just as it is written and forever remains written,

"For Your sake we are put to death all day long;

We are regarded as sheep for the slaughter."

37 Yet in all these things we are more than conquerors and gain an overwhelming victory through Him who loved us [so much that He died for us]. 38 For I am convinced [and continue to be convinced—beyond any doubt] that neither death, nor life, nor angels, nor principalities, nor things present and threatening, nor things to come, nor powers, 39 nor height, nor depth, nor any other created thing, will be able to separate us from the [unlimited] love of God, which is in Christ Jesus our Lord. (Romans 8:31–39) AMB

When we have Christ Jesus in our hearts, we gain the strength we need to be courageous and victorious in life.

"But thanks be to God, who gives us the victory [as conquerors] through our Lord Jesus Christ." 1 Corinthians 15:57 AMB

I discovered God's magnificent love. - It is called unconditional love. - I keep it very deeply in my heart, as the most beautiful and precious treasure I have ever had.

Guard [with greatest care] and keep unchanged, the treasure [that precious truth] which has been entrusted to you [that is, the good news about salvation through personal faith in Christ Jesus], through [the help of] the Holy Spirit who dwells in us. (2 Timothy 1:14) AMB

We all have a purpose in life. - We are part of an extraordinary story. - We are the pages of the Book of His creation. - We are part of the movie of life. - We are small pieces that make up a big puzzle that comes together to form the body of Christ. - Scripture says: we are courageous, we are victorious, we are beautiful, we are valuable, we are the apple of His eye, we are wonderful, we love people, we are perfect in God's eyes, we are strong, we have wisdom, and we are intelligent, among other names. - Jesus created us with His loving hands, blowing into our nostrils the breath of life, giving us the spirit to live, and we become human beings, formed in His image. - Only God can create the spirit of any human being.

Only God can call us by our name, and redirect the course of our lives in the way He sees fit. - Only God can give us an amazing, perfect creation in His universe. - Only God can call us children, no matter our imperfections. I found the true purpose of life, a purpose that I can only describe with one word: ***Holiness.***

[a]Therefore I urge you, [b]brothers and sisters, by the mercies of God, to present your bodies [dedicating all of yourselves, set apart] as a living sacrifice, holy and well-pleasing to God, which is your rational (logical, intelligent) act of worship. 2 And do not be conformed to this world [any longer with its superficial values and customs], but be [c]transformed and progressively changed [as you mature spiritually] by the renewing of your mind [focusing on godly values and ethical attitudes], so that you may prove [for yourselves] what the will of God is, that which is good and acceptable and perfect [in His plan and purpose for you]. (Romans 12:1–2) AMB

The least we can do in return for God's love is to develop a holy and friendly relationship with Jesus. - That way, we can begin to bear the fruit of the Spirit and allow our hearts to express real and true love for God.

But the fruit of the Spirit [the result of His presence within us] is Love [unselfish concern for others], joy, [inner] peace, patience [not the ability to wait, but how we act while waiting], kindness, goodness, faithfulness, 23 gentleness, self-control. Against such things, there is no law. (Galatians 5:22–23) AMB

When your heart begins to bear the fruit of the Spirit, it is the most splendid feeling your being can experience. - It is the victory of all your efforts. - It is the triumph of your suffering but, more importantly, the real understanding of your life. - Living in holiness is the real reason for our existence, and it is God's will. - I had a real encounter with Jesus Christ. - It was a change of life. -

Jesus answered, "I assure you and most solemnly say to you, unless one is born of water and the Spirit, he cannot [ever] enter the kingdom of God. 6 That which is born of the flesh is flesh [the physical is merely physical], and that which is born of The Spirit is spirit. 7 Do not be surprised that I have told you, 'You must be born again [reborn from above—spiritually transformed, renewed, sanctified].' - (John 3: 5-7) AMB

Jesus said we must be born again, and that is what happened to me. - I was born again; except this time, I died physically and spiritually as well. - Jesus saved me from hell. - He gave me a new Spirit and a new life within me. - He dwells within me, and today I can enjoy the mind, heart, and Spirit of Jesus Christ. - He forgave me, and I forgave all the people who hurt me. - New life! - a new beginning! - new dreams! - Thank You, Lord! -

You do not need to die physically, as I did, to be born again.

The Bible says that

"Because if you acknowledge and confess with your mouth that Jesus is Lord [recognizing His power, authority, and majesty as God], and believe in your heart that God raised Him from the dead, you will be saved.

10 For with the heart a person believes [in Christ as Savior] resulting in his justification [that is, being made righteous—being freed of the guilt of sin and made acceptable to God]; and with the mouth he

acknowledges and confesses [his faith openly], resulting in and confirming [his] salvation. - (Romans 10:9–10) AMB

When you receive Jesus Christ as your God and Savior into your heart, you are spiritually born again.

- Are you ready to start a new life, having the Holy Spirit within you?

___

- Do you want to change the course of your life by walking forward, not backwards ________ - Are you ready to give your life to Jesus Christ, hoping that He will give you something better in return?

___

- Do you trust the Lord?

___

- Do you want Him to be a part of your life?

___

- Do you want to have peace and joy in your heart all the time?

___

If you are ready, let the Spirit of the Lord into your heart! - Open your heart and just believe that amazing things will happen in your life after this.

Once you surrender your life to Jesus Christ, the true and only living God, seek out a Christian church and be baptized with water to be genuinely called a son or daughter of God. - Trust me, after you begin to experience the Holy Spirit within you, a new chapter will take place in your life; everything will be new: you will have a new heart, a new beginning, a new mind, new Blessings, new opportunities, new wisdom, new intelligence, new knowledge, new spirit, everything will be renewed.

Eternal life Lasts Forever

- After Jesus reveals to you the true purpose of your life, everything will be different. - You will begin to live in Heaven, here on earth. That is when eternal life begins! - It is time to turn the page on the sad and doomed and spiritual confusion of the story you have lived, and begin to live a wonderful, joyful, and peaceful life with the Spirit of Jesus Christ in your heart. -

If you have decided to give your life to the Lord, I want to welcome you to the new life in Christ. - Welcome to the new family of Jesus Christ! - It was the best decision you ever made. - Welcome to Heaven and eternal life! - "Eternal life lasts forever!" - I would love to hear your new story on my new website and how the prayer of salvation changed your life. -

Share your true testimony with others on my website at authoressadrianabrunga.com

Let us pray together a prayer of Salvation. - Say it out loud, with an open and sincere heart.

Beloved Father, I love You. - I believe that Jesus Christ is the Son of God. - I repent of my sins. I think someone had to pay for my sins. - I believe that Jesus Christ rose from the dead and is seated today at the right hand of the Heavenly Father, God. - I accept Him as my Savior and Lord. I accept Him as payment for my sins. - I put all my trust in what He did for me. - I do not trust what I can do anymore. Thank You, Lord, for receiving me into Your family and putting me in the Book of life. - In Jesus' name, I pray. - Amen.

Chapter 3

The Divine Journey: Navigating into the Birth and Death of the Soul

'Do not fear [anything], for I am with you;
Do not be afraid, for I am your God.

I will strengthen you, be assured I will help you;
I will certainly take hold of you with My righteous right hand [a hand of justice, of power, of victory, of salvation].'

—Isaiah 41:10 (AMB)

I have been exposed to the hands of the Devil many times as long as I can remember. - My dad taking out his anger on my mom for no reason was the most abrupt action I could ever understand. - I was sexually molested in my younger years, but even so, I was able to identify the darkness in people's hearts, and the fearful world we lived in. I was afraid to tell my parents, or even anyone, about the abuse because I did not know what their reaction would be. -

God knew the reason why He created me in life. - He never failed me. - Regardless of the circumstances I had to endure, I thanked God for His love and protection. - God was my cornerstone, my secret place to hide, and my comfort, and peace, in days of need. - Three years later, after my surgery in 2009, the enemy again tried to attack my life. - The first time

I ran away from home, I was in the room with my daughter, Sarah, and a soft voice came to me saying, "Run". - I quickly looked at Sarah, feeling confused and desperate, but soon, I started running away from home. -

I found myself in the middle of Highway one sixty, a half mile from home, looking for my dad, who had died twenty-four years earlier. - I was shouting, "Where are you? -Where are you, dad?" - He did not listen to me. No one could help me. I found myself surrounded by woods in the dark. I searched for my dad for an hour, but I did not get a response from anyone. At that moment, in my spirit, I was looking at my dad being kidnapped, tortured, and murdered. Milton found me thirty minutes later. He quickly put me in the car and took me back home. I was crying, heartbroken, and I hurriedly locked myself in the closet. I called my cousin Luz in Colombia, South America, and I described to her where my dad was hiding when he was murdered. -

I was totally terrified. - The next day, I woke up with severe pain all over my body, and I could not move or walk. - The same episode occurred again, six months later. - I ran away from home for the second time. - I found myself running in the middle of Highway one sixty. My mother found me there. - She tried to stop me several times but could not do it. - I kept screaming, calling for help as I desperately searched for my dad. I explained where he was buried, but no one understood me. - Soon, the police showed up, and they put me in the patrol car, handcuffed for a while. - My mother was crying terribly, calling me "Nana." -

"Nana, please talk to me." - I could not recognize her; I did not know who my mother was. - Minutes later, my husband appeared and said, "Honey, look at me." - I could not recognize him either. I felt very strange; the whole world had stopped at me. - My feelings and emotions were focused on finding my dad. - My mind was absent from my body. - I saw everything in slow motion. - I felt like my body was present at that moment, but my thoughts were captured in the past. - Unexpectedly, I tried to break the police computer inside the car. - I grabbed the rifle, but the rifle was jammed. - The police officer immediately took me to the hospital. - When I arrived at the hospital, they sedated me and moved me to a restricted area. -

They put me under supervision for twenty-four hours. I woke up screaming, "Where is my dad? - Where is my dad? - The nurse approached me and asked: "What happened, Adriana?" - No one could understand why I was acting like this. Two years later, in October 2014, I ended up in a psychiatric hospital. I had "Conversion Disorder", a post-traumatic stress disorder, but this was more than "Conversion Disorder". - I found myself walking in the hallway. Talking to myself; I experienced a severe personality disorder. - Suddenly, I was running in the hallway. - It was around nine at night. - I ran non-stop in the hospital, since I felt that someone was chasing me to kill me. -

I screamed for help. - I was looking for my dad, but no one knew where he was. I went to my room, and my roommate, Mary, offered to pray with me. - But my level of anxiety and persecution was stronger than anything I could control at that moment. - That night, something unforgettable happened. - They left me alone in my bedroom. - I was on the ground, crying with deep pain in my heart. - I saw a girl who was crying, but the girl was me.

- I was crying for my dad. - I could see how he was killed. - I was begging for help from anyone, but I could only see it in my spirit. - I cried and asked for help. - I screamed, with deep pain in my heart, but there was no one around. - I was terrified to see his murder. Minutes later, my roommate, Mary, appeared in the room with the rest of the patients.

They hugged me and told me: "You will be fine soon, Adriana." - At that moment, I found myself in the little house that I had always dreamed of since I was a child. I realized that I was in the middle of a storm and had sought refuge in that little house, protected by God. I cried and cried, letting out all my feelings. It looked like I was passing through a tornado; I was in the middle, while the wind was destroying everything around me. - That was the tornado I had feared my entire life. -

For years, I lived with scared emotions and could not face the true giant of my life. - That was the real reality I had to face to be delivered from the hands of the enemy (Satan). - The giants I had to face were terror and fear; those are spirits of Satan. Those spirits paralyzed my emotions, causing me to act irrationally, to the point where I thought wrong was right. - The next day, I understood about the day my dad was murdered. - He grabbed me, and he did not let me go, because he loved me so much. - Six months later, the symptoms of "Conversion Disorder" worsened daily. -

I called my friend Pastor Yeimy in Colombia to pray for me. - She delivered me from the hands of the enemy with a spiritual deliverance. - The enemy tried to kill me in many ways, but the Lord's protection was greater than that. - I was in the hands of the enemy (the Devil) most of my life, probably from the moment I was born. - The only thing that kept me strong was the promise of God in my heart. -

The enemy's plan was to destroy and kill me, but God's grace and my faith in Him was enough for me.

I can do all things [which He has called me to do] through Him who strengthens and empowers me [to fulfill His purpose—I am self-sufficient in Christ's sufficiency; I am ready for anything and equal to anything through Him who infuses me with inner strength and confident peace.] (Philippians 4:13) AMB

My heart was filled with fear and terror. - I never knew I would have to face the enemy the way I did. I never knew that the enemy was using my soul (thoughts, emotions, will, and feelings) to destroy me. No matter how many things I saw in life or how much emotional pain I had to endure, today, I can say that I am free from the hands of the enemy, free from condemnation; free from hate; free from any diabolical attack; free from the past! I am a new creature in Christ. I was born again fifteen years ago, and today, I live my life full of victory and love.

"The Spirit of the Lord is upon Me (the Messiah),

Because He has anointed Me to preach the good news to the poor. He has sent Me to announce release (pardon, forgiveness) to the captives, and recovery of sight to the blind, to set free those who are oppressed (downtrodden, bruised, crushed by tragedy), 19 to proclaim the favorable year of the Lord [the day when salvation and the favor of God abound greatly]." ... (Luke 4:18–19) AMB

I could not identify the Devil's attack upon me, before entering the presence of the Lord. - All my thoughts, emotions, will, and feelings (soul), and actions seemed to be normal. - For many years, I thought this behavior was normal. - Years later, I discovered that as soon as you receive Jesus as your Lord and Savior, the enemy tries to prevent you from fulfilling God's calling. -

The greater the call from God, the more spiritual attacks you will receive from Satan. - Jesus had a big job to do with me. - I was trapped in trauma for most of my life, not knowing how the Devil worked. - Satan keeps me thinking the same thoughts over and over, like a video tape in my mind, making me feel condemned and guilty for something that was not my fault. It is part of the circumstances that I must live in at that moment. -Finally, Jesus Christ brought me out of this trauma. -

He forgave me and made me complete in Him. I finally made peace with my past and present. - Today, I live a Blessed and joyful life. - I have no words to express my immense gratitude to the Lord for saving me, and, most importantly, for allowing me to see the face of the enemy and understand how Satan works in people's minds. -

- Do you identify with my circumstances?

____

- Do you feel condemned and guilty for your past?

____

- Are you stuck in your past and cannot seem to move forward?

____

- Does your mind play the same video tape over and over again?

____

- Do you find it difficult to forgive those who hurt you?

- Do you feel trapped in a spiritual battle?

Well, those are signs that the Devil is trying to keep you attached to those memories. This is called a spiritual attack.

- The Devil's job is to destroy your emotions, steal your thoughts, kill your feelings, and ultimately win your will and soul. - He knows that if you do not have peace of mind, your emotions are upside down, and your feelings are hurt. - He can use you to do terrible things against others, to hate and even kill people, because your soul is corrupted by him. - Know that by keeping your thoughts attached to the past, it can fuel more resentment and anger toward others, causing you to act irrationally. - You cannot fix your past; only Jesus can do that because there is spiritual damage, due to all the bad experiences in your life. -

I do not blame you for feeling this way. - I was like that, too, at one point in my life, but I always believed in God. - I have loved Jesus since I was six years old, not knowing that He was the true living God. - If you have not accepted Jesus as your Lord and Savior, I advise you to do so. - Everything will change for the better, and you will finally understand why you had to live the experiences you had in your past. - The spiritual separation that we had from God from the moment we were born, due to the original sin that Adam and Eve had committed, will help us better understand life and realize that apart from God, we can do nothing. - This will help us appreciate life better. -

You will also be able to identify the good (Jesus) and the bad (the Devil). - You will grow even more as a person. - You will open your mind to a different dimension, and you will even thank God for all the bad experiences you have had because wisdom will take place. - I concluded that traumas or bad circumstances are necessary in our lives. Thanks to those experiences, we can understand life better. - God uses your bad experiences for His own good. - He is an expert in using bad experiences and turning them into a good life scenario in your life. - As He promised us, He will pay you double for your trouble. - You will see how Jesus Christ will Bless you with a double portion in every problem you have had, so that, in the end, it will turn out well for you. -

As soon as you give your life to Jesus and begin an intimate relationship with the Lord, He will reveal the truth to you, and the truth will set you free, as the Bible says. - The Lord is an expert at using the bad circumstances in your life and turning them to your advantage. - Everything works for the good of the Lord. -

The Scriptures say that the Lord will pay us double for every problem we suffer in life: double joy, double love, double Blessing, double peace.

Instead of your [former] shame you will have a [a]double portion; And instead of humiliation your people will shout for joy over their portion. Therefore, in their land they will possess double [what they had forfeited]; Everlasting joy will be theirs. (Isaiah 61:7) AMB

Let us pray together,

Father, I love You. You know I was under attack from the Devil. - You know what I had to go through in life and the terrifying fear I held in my heart. - God, only You know the great plans you have for my life, plans of salvation and the Light of Jesus Christ. - The enemy tried to destroy me many times, taking my life. - Thank You, Lord, for delivering me! Thank You for the forgiveness, strength, and courage You gave me. I am free, Lord; I am free! - Thank You for Your powerful protection over me. - Please continue protecting me from any evil attacks. - If You have taken me this far, it is because of Your Almighty reason, which only You know, Lord. - The enemy tried to destroy me many times, but You knew I had to pass this test to be saved by Jesus Christ. -

“And we [have seen and] know [by personal experience] that the Son of God has [actually] come [to this world], and has given us understanding and insight so that we may [progressively and personally] know Him who is true; and we are in Him who is true—in His Son Jesus Christ. This is the true God and eternal life.” (1 John 5:20). AMB

In the name of Jesus, I pray. - Amen.

Chapter 4

Undermarking the Enemy: Understanding the Devil's Tactic

Jose Geovany Pineda
(January 17, 1995 – December 17, 2019)

By Your favor and grace, O Lord, you have made my mountain stand strong;
You hid Your face, and I was horrified. —

Psalm 30:7 (AMB)

Be sober [well balanced and self-disciplined], be alert and cautious at all times. That enemy of yours, the devil, prowls around like a roaring lion [fiercely hungry], seeking someone to devour. 9 But resist him, be firm in your faith [against his attack—rooted, established, immovable], knowing that the same experiences of suffering are being experienced by your brothers and sisters throughout the world. [You do not suffer alone.] - —

1 Peter 5:8-9 (AMB)

Having been under attack by the Devil in the past, I realized that we are experiencing a spiritual war. - As warriors of God, our duty is to help people in any spiritual need of Jesus Christ, the true living God. - The Lord has anointed us in various ways to be successful gladiators of God's ministry. - We must be alert to identify the Devil's trap. - The Devil attacks our Spirit, making us do the opposite of God's will. I will put on the full armor of God (the armor of a heavily armed soldier, which God provides) to be able to successfully confront all the Devil's schemes and deceptions.

Put on the full armor of God [for His precepts are like the splendid armor of a heavily armed soldier], so that you may be able to [successfully] stand up against all the schemes and the strategies and the deceits of the devil. 12 For our struggle is not against flesh and blood [contending only with physical opponents], but against the rulers, against the powers, against the world forces of this [present] darkness, against the spiritual forces of wickedness in the Heavenly (supernatural) places. 13 Therefore, put on the complete armor of God, so that you will be able to [successfully] resist and stand your ground in the evil day [of danger], and having done everything [that the crisis demands], to stand firm [in your place, fully prepared, immovable, victorious]. 14 So stand firm and hold your ground, having [a]tightened the wide band of truth (personal integrity, moral courage) around your waist and having put on the breastplate of righteousness (an upright heart), 15 and having [b]strapped on your feet the gospel of peace in preparation [to face the enemy with firm-footed stability and the readiness produced by the good news]. 16 Above all, lift up the [protective] [c]shield of faith with which you can extinguish all the flaming arrows of the evil one. 17 And take the helmet of salvation, and the sword of the Spirit, which is the Word of God. (Ephesians 6:11–17) AMB

When I was a child, - I was confused, I had many thoughts in my mind. - Many dreams that God planted in my heart as a child allowed me to see victory and triumph ahead of time. - Those dreams were promises from God. Thirty-two years later, I had received many of those promises that I called “Blessings.” God is the author of the Book of life.

As time goes by, God continues to reveal to me, little by little, the plans he has for me. No matter how many wrong decisions we make, how many times we disobey Him, or how many times we go against Him, He is the only one who can direct us to the right path because He is our Creator. -

Jesus Christ is a specialist who brings good things out of bad experiences. - Every time we experience some difficulty, economic situation, adversity or injustice, it is a sign that a Blessing is on the way. Do not be discouraged! - Instead, thank God for all the adversities you have had to endure and allow the Blessings to come into your life.

We all have a purpose; We all have a story to tell; We all have a destiny to fulfill. - God did not create you to just work, or to let you go through the adversities of life. His main purpose is for us to multiply (have children, reproduce our Godly behavior), be fruitful (reproduce the fruit of the Spirit, live in the Spirit), and live in Holiness (have God as a priority in everything we do in the life; being connected with God all the time). - What does it really mean to be fruitful or live in Holiness? - It means that God is more interested in us bearing fruit than in us working, being stressed, or loving what the world offers us.

But the fruit of the Spirit [the result of His presence within us] is love [unselfish concern for others], joy, [inner] peace, patience [not the ability to wait, but how we act while waiting], kindness, goodness, faithfulness, 23 gentleness, self-control. Against such things, there is no law. (Galatians 5:22–23) AMB

God promised that we would have great opportunities in life; in fact, He promised not to leave us alone or abandon us. - Today, we can be Blessed with great opportunities available in life.

The Scriptures tell us: 12 So, as God's own chosen people, who are holy [set apart, sanctified for His purpose] and well-beloved [by God Himself], put on a heart of compassion, kindness, humility, gentleness, and patience [which has the power to endure whatever injustice or unpleasantness comes, with good temper]; 13 bearing graciously with one another, and willingly forgiving each other if one has a cause for complaint against another; just as the Lord has forgiven you, so should you forgive. 14 Beyond all these things, put on and wrap yourselves in [unselfish] love, which is the perfect bond of unity [for everything is bound together in agreement when each one seeks the best for others]. 15 Let the peace of Christ [the inner calm of one who walks daily with Him] be the controlling factor in your hearts [deciding and settling questions that arise]. To this peace indeed, you were called as members in one body [of believers]. And be thankful [to God always]. (Colossians 3:12–15) AMB

That is the armor of God that we must wear every day to please the Lord and combat the Devil's trap. - We are living in a spiritual war. - We are not here to fight against each other; We are here to show the good behavior of God through Jesus Christ. - I realized that God has protected me all these years for a reason, even amid danger. - He called me to the ministry of God, long before I was born, using it to display God's principles.

He created me for a greater purpose that only He knows. I endured a lot of spiritual pain in my soul (emotions, thoughts, will, feelings). In fact, I have lived most of my life with a broken heart, but only God restored me and made me whole, a new creature in Christ. God allowed many injustices to happen to me, but He never left me unprotected or alone. -

He equipped me with the right strength, courage, and wisdom to understand the difference between good and evil. - The enemy (Devil) is here to destroy God's creation. - He is the father of lies. - He has power, but only Jesus Christ, the true living God, has the final authority. - God put the fruit of the seeds of the Spirit in my heart to develop me. - He has given me the wisdom to identify good and evil since I was eight years old.

The Spirit of the Lord God is upon me, Because the Lord has anointed and commissioned me to bring good news to the humble and afflicted; He has sent me to bind up [the wounds of] the brokenhearted, to proclaim release [from confinement and condemnation] to the [physical and spiritual] captives and freedom to prisoners, - (Isaiah 61:1) AMB

After losing my life in the hospital, the next day, I saw a great vision before my eyes. I saw my dad in a big hole (mass grave), where he was buried after being murdered, asking me for help. He was full of life but covered in mud and dust. - I quickly extended my hand, helping him out of that hole. - He had a big smile on his face. Driving home with my mom, I described the vision I had seen, and she exclaimed, "Daughter, that was the hole your dad dug for many years, leading to destruction and the end of his life."

What does this really mean? - It means we have the choice in our hands. - We can obey God, listening to His small voice whispering in our ears, so that we understand what is good, and what is evil, and do not risk our lives; or we can choose to follow the broad path that will lead us to death, destroying our life spiritually or even physically.

- What hole are you digging today?

___

- Is it a drug addiction?

___

- Alcohol abuse?

___

- Sexual immorality?

___

- Infidelity?

___

- Iniquity?

___

- Corruption?

___

-Which one is it?

___

Whatever it is, this will only lead you down the path of destruction, leaving you dead yet alive (spiritually death). When we sin, when we are disobedient or do contrary to God's will, we only harm ourselves because God does not see the sin in us. - He keeps us separated from Him (apart from Holiness) automatically. - God calls us to live in the Spirit - live in Holiness (Set apart for God) He calls us to bear fruit (fruit of the Spirit). - He calls us to fulfill the dreams he has for our lives (visions). He gave us this beautiful world to enjoy until it was time to leave for a better life (reborn spiritually or born again).

I have seen the protection that God has given me my entire life. - I can see how much He loved me, showing me Mercy and compassion in times of adversity. I was exposed to difficult times, but

He continued to put dreams of victory in my heart. - Little by little, those dreams come true, making me feel happy.

I crossed the line of life (stormy death/spiritual death) and reached the goal (proof of life). I am finally living eternal life (i.e., living for eternity with the Lord) while I am still alive, living in Holiness with God - being close to God, being in the Spirit, bearing fruit (exercising the fruit of the Spirit; - (See Galatians 5:22) that allows me to be joyful and at peace in Christ.

16 But I say, walk habitually in the [Holy] Spirit [seek Him and be responsive to His guidance], and then you will certainly not carry out the desire of the [a]sinful nature [which responds impulsively without regard for God and His precepts]. 17 For the sinful nature has its desire which is opposed to the Spirit, and the [desire of the] Spirit opposes the [b]sinful nature; for these, [two, the sinful nature and the Spirit] are in direct opposition to each other [continually in conflict], so that you [as believers] do not [always] do whatever [good things] you want to do. 18 But if you are guided and led by the Spirit, you are not subject to the Law. (Galatians 5:16–18). AMB

For many years, I lived my life in the flesh (carnal desires), not knowing what God had prepared for my life. - Today, I clearly understand that being obedient to God is much better than not doing so because life is full of opportunities that we miss, because we have not listened to the gentle whisper of God. I lived under condemnation most of my life, holding the guilt of my dad's death in my heart, not realizing that it was not my fault. - It was his own choice because he wanted to help his friend whose wife was kidnapped.

Every action has a reaction

He exposed his life to the end. - He died helping a friend, without knowing that his friend worked for Pablo Escobar, which got us all into something, and we did not know what was happening. Thank God nothing happened to us. - We pay the consequences of our actions in life.

Every action has a reaction. - We do not need to die to start living in the Promised Land. - The beginning of our eternal life begins here on earth, living in Christ, and putting on the armor of God to defeat the attack of the enemy (spiritual warfare).

Now, a second reality has crossed my life again. - For twenty-four years, exactly the life cycle of my son Jose, I lived my life thinking that I was responsible for my dad's death. After seeking psychiatric and psychological help, I finally understood that I was not responsible for my dad's death; It was just a circumstance that had to be experienced at that time. - After overcoming this horrible trauma before Jesus Christ appeared in my life, a third test was presented to me, and this time, it was even worse than the first. Words cannot describe, feelings cannot feel, emotions cannot express, and thoughts cannot even imagine. - This is called spiritual soul, soul-breaking or spiritual breaking.

It was the death of my eldest son, Jose Geovany Pineda. - He was only twenty-four years old. - The first test I had to go through was the death of my dad (first trauma); The second test I had to go through was the injury to my lower back and neck (unexplained, drastic, and traumatic physical pain, surpassing any strong pain). - And the third test I had to go through (second trauma) was the death of my own son.

Words cannot even explain, but this time, Jesus Christ was by my side. - The Death of My Firstborn, precisely thirty years after my dad's death, and that was my dad's age when he was killed, my son's life was taken in an incredibly sad way. He was helping the wrong person at the wrong time.

On December 17, 2019, at 3:05 AM in the morning, my son was pronounced dead in a lonely parking lot.

It all started on Thanksgiving Day, November 26, 2019. My son had come to my house to celebrate Thanksgiving with the family and me. That day, we found out that he was helping a friend (a girl) who was homeless. - He told me about it, and I found it really kind of him. - I asked him many times if he knew this girl, Sophie. - He said, "Yes, mom. - I have known her for a while. We did not see anything wrong in this because we always told him that he would help those in need. - He was a good and kind person, and we always trusted him with his friends.

He said he would help her for a month, so it was not a problem for us. - "If it is for that short period of time, it is fine," I said. - On December 15, 2019, he decided to bring this girl to our house to meet us. - This was two days before his death. - I told him it was a good idea, so he drove from his house, which was about an hour from my house. - It was around six in the afternoon when we received a phone call from the police department, informing us that my son had been in a car accident.

My son was in the military, but he was on permanent disability because he had epileptic seizures. That day, when I was driving home, he had an epileptic seizure attack. He was rushed to the hospital. - We all went to the hospital to see him. - Thank God, nothing important happened to him or anyone else that day, other than destroying his car in the accident. I was there with this girl, who seemed genuinely nice and kind. - However, her physical appearance was that of a person addicted to drugs.

My daughter said, “Mom, I think she is weird.” - And I answered: “Yes, daughter, but we cannot judge by physical appearance. We must see her heart. - They spent the entire weekend at my daughter's house. - I only saw her for three hours that day. My daughter told me, after my son's death, that Sophie acted differently on Saturday than when we saw her on Friday. On Saturday, Sophie’s behavior was irrational and strange. My daughter told my son not to have this person in his house anymore, for the sake of him and the children. - My son took my daughter's car for a week since he did not have a car, due to the car accident he had on Friday.

Monday, December 16, 2019, just a month before my son's birthday, was my daughter's graduation from the University of South Carolina. - She graduated with a degree in criminal justice after four years of college. - That day, the entire family gathered to attend her graduation. - We were incredibly happy, honored, and overjoyed by my daughter's achievement. - At seven at night, we said goodbye to my son Jose, and we all went to our hometown to celebrate my daughter's graduation in a restaurant. - Jose spoke to Milton, his dad, at eleven forty-five at night, telling him that he was not feeling well and that he wanted to take the day off from school the next day. - Milton said, "Yes, son, take the day off. He answered". My son was the most amazing, smart, kind, excellent student and the best person ever. He was one year away from graduating from college.

At first, he studied aerospace engineering, but after having his two children, he had to change his career for another. He was going through a divorce and had two sons: Joey, three years old, and Michael, two years old, whom he loved his entire life. - I could not see a better dad than him. - We do not know what happened that night when he was talking to Sophie; All we know is that Milton received a phone call from the police department at eleven the next morning, telling him that our son was dead. My sister, Laura, was driving me to the Doctor's office that day, and my daughter called me. - "Mom! Jose is dead!" I felt like the whole world had collapsed on me for a second. I was still speechless, and my heart stopped beating for a second. I was confused, feeling no emotions, as the burning sensation of a pointed arrow pierced my heart, breaking every part of it.

- After a few seconds, I yelled, "Tell me no! Lord, this is not true. - This is not possible. - "My son cannot be dead!" - I got out of the car. - There was mud on the wet grass. - That day was dark and rainy. - I screamed, looking up at the sky. - "Why, Jesus? - Why, my son, Lord?" - No, tell me my son is not dead, Jesus! - What happened to the angels? - I have prayed every day for the protection of my children. What happened to my son, Lord?"- I was going crazy, screaming like a madman and senseless in the middle of the road, in the same place where I had looked for my dad, years before. Many people stopped to help us, but I was uncontrollable. - I asked the Lord, with my heart broken into pieces, "Why did my son have to die, Lord?" - An arrow pierced my heart; I had never felt so much pain. - It was the most painful spiritual pain I had ever endured.

I thought my dad's death was painful, until that day. - Why did my son have to die, Jesus? - Why? - Why? - Why? - I was just shouting, looking at the sky, waiting for a response, but I got no response. - I wanted answers, but the Lord remained silent. - My sister was heartbroken. - We did not know what to do. My sister, Laura, and I, with a lady who stopped to help us, took my sister and I home. - It was wet and had mud everywhere. They called an ambulance because I was not well. Immediately, I had "Conversion Disorder." - I acted and talked like a three-year-old girl.

- The paramedics came to my house, but they wanted to take me to the hospital. - I refused to go there because I wanted to see and touch my son directly, to pray for a resurrection. - I was completely convinced and assured in faith that if I touched my son and prayed at that moment, he could live again, as I had done five times before. I was hoping for a miracle from Jesus, but the police did not let us see my son until a week later. - I ended up having "Conversion Disorder", for six hours.

Only God knows the deep, spiritual, and agonizing pain that my family and I had to endure those days. We all ended up together for fourteen days until we buried my son on December 31, 2019. We could only hear a deep, deep silence in the house; It was the deepest painful grief we had ever experienced in our lives. - The deep and sincere sound of death was the only meaning. - I believe in the justice of the Lord, and in due time, God will provide justice for my son Jose. - It took me seven months to come back to reality after trying to kill myself four times. - Jesus saved my life again. - It felt like we were in a movie; everything moved in terrible slow motion (a sign of trauma).

However, the Devil used someone we trusted to take my son's life. - Today, after all the spiritual suffering we had, I feel restored and full of joy again, knowing that Jesus never left me alone. - Instead, He explained to me what had happened and why he rescued my son's spirit that day. - At this moment, I can feel at peace, knowing that my son is with the Lord, only because he was baptized and received Jesus Christ into his heart as his Savior and Lord, many years before that day.

Thanks to my son Jose Pineda, I was saved by the Lord and received the Lord as my Savior and God in my heart on the same day as my other son, Diego Pineda. - My son Jose did not know much about the evil and malicious way the spirit of darkness uses people's minds. He grew up in a happy home with a good environment, surrounded by good people. - He did not know that by helping this person he was risking his life, neither did we, but we learned a great lesson from that experience.

With her many persuasions, she caused him to yield; With her flattering lips, she seduced him. 22 Suddenly he went after her, as an ox goes to the slaughter [not knowing the outcome], Or as one in stocks going to the correction [to be given] to a fool, 23 Until an arrow pierced his liver [with a mortal wound]; Like a bird fluttering straight into the net, He did not know that it would cost him his life. 24 Now, therefore, my sons listen to me, and pay attention to the words of my mouth. 25 Do not let your heart turn aside to her ways, do not stray into her [evil, immoral] paths. 26 For she has cast down many [mortally] wounded; Indeed, all who were killed by her were strong. 27 - Her house is the way to [a]Shoal, Descending to the chambers of death. (Proverbs 7:21–27) AMB

Pay attention, young people. - Read Proverbs of King Solomon in the Bible. Do not let your carnal desires and hearts weaken with women like this. - Their only intention is to steal you, destroy you, and finally kill you. - They possess the spirit of darkness (Satan). - Be wise and listen to the Lord and His commandments.

- Why expose yourself like this to the Devil's hand?

____

- Is it worth helping the wrong person?

____

- Will it bring you any benefits?

____

Not at all. - On the contrary, it can lead to destruction and death.

Be wise; protect your life. - Ask your parents, a Pastor, or any spiritual person for any advice you may need. - Ask, just ask. - They are the right people to help you save your life. From a spiritual point of view, this type of woman sells her body to different idols and is possessed by the spirit of darkness within her heart, and if you ignore the truth of the Bible, it can lead to spiritual destruction or death.

Thank God that today, Jesus Christ has healed me again; the true living God is there. - I prayed during my agony that he would not leave me alone, that he would not abandon me for even a second. - Even amid my despair and pain, when I made many mistakes during the healing test, He never left me alone. - I am healed in His Almighty name. I thank Him for my life, because I realized that my other two children, and grandchildren, needed me too. - I thank the Lord, who allowed me to share this story with joy and love. - I hope to help someone in need who has had a spiritual breakdown or has suffered some spiritual rupture.

Especially for those parents who have lost their child, I can clearly and honestly understand your deep spiritual pain, your deep agonizing pain that your heart feels today, but I prayed to the Lord for your restoration and healing in your heart. - Trust me; He will restore you. - He will heal you so that you will never feel that horrible pain in your heart again. - He is faithful. - He is loyal to His promises. He is God. Do not let go of Him! - I love You, Jesus, and thank You for never leaving me alone or helpless, not even for a second. Best of all, thank You for the complete restoration my heart has received today, with Your great power.

After receiving a complete restoration from Jesus Christ, I finally understood that we are living in a spiritual war, and we need to fight back with prayers and the full armor of God, and confront the Devil, and the spiritual forces that come from the darkness, with the sword of the Spirit, the Word of God. Jesus made me an active gladiator and warrior in the spiritual field. - Now, I am not afraid of Satan. - I saw the enemy face to face, and now even hell can shake and stumble when it hears my name.

I became a spiritual warrior with no compassion for Satan's plans. - The spirit of darkness will be afraid of the full authority that Jesus gave me in the spiritual field because the Lord prepared me to be one of His best soldiers.

Jesus said, "I have given you full authority to cast out demons and powerful forces in darkness."

Unfortunately, I was too spiritually weak to understand this or act on it when I met Sophie. - The day of judgment for Jesus Christ is approaching, because He is our Creator.

Eternal life Lasts Forever

He is the Beginning and the End. - I leave everything in the hands of God, because her day will come, and I will see it. - God is faithful, and He is loyal to His promises.

Unfortunately, I lost my precious son Jose, an extraordinary son and dad, but today, he is with our God, Jesus Christ, the true living God, enjoying His presence in full peace and joy.

One day, I will see him again. One day, I will have him in my arms, and this time for all eternity. - Eternity is longer than life; It never ends. Life is temporary and always has its due time. - I do not let my feelings control my emotions or deny God's promises. Today, I can safely say that I have forgiven this girl. She was used by the Devil, and she is not a daughter of God.

She thinks her actions are right and ignores her irrational actions. I ask the Lord to have mercy on her because she will need it. - Hell is for eternity, and it is not pleasant to be there. - However, eternal life is for eternity and endures forever! - And it is so nice to be there in the presence of the Lord. - "Eternal life lasts forever!"

Let us pray together,

Heavenly Father, I love You. - I want to put on the armor of God every day. - I want to walk in the Spirit, pleasing You excessively all the time. - Please forgive me for being disobedient to You and turning away from You many times. Jesus You are my savior. - You are the Light that illuminates my path. - Please bring me closer to You every day. - Show me the way to follow Your steps, to be an example for many people, reflecting God's principles.

Thank You, Lord, for listening to my prayers. - I understand that we are living a spiritual war that only You can help me win. - Thank You for choosing me to be here on this earth and be a representative of Your love. I pray for all parents who have lost their precious children. - Please touch their hearts and give them the complete restoration, and peace they need, so that one day, they can live in peace, and joy, with Your presence and enjoy life again. - Please protect me from any evil attack, and let me walk with Your Son, Jesus Christ. - In the name of Jesus, I pray. Amen.

Part Number Two
Scene Two: When the Enemy Attacks

Chapter 5

New Beginning: Walking in Freedom and Purpose with Jesus Christ

16 So from now on, we regard no one from a human point of view [according to worldly standards and values]. Though we have known Christ from a human point of view, now we no longer know Him in this way. 17 Therefore, if anyone is in Christ [that is, grafted in, joined to Him by faith in Him as Savior], he is a new creature [reborn and renewed by the Holy Spirit]; the old things [the previous moral and spiritual condition] have passed away. Behold, new things have come [because spiritual awakening brings a new life]. —

2 Corinthians 5:16–17 (AMB)

17 Now the Lord is the Spirit, and where the Spirit of the Lord is, there is liberty [emancipation from bondage, true freedom]. — 2 Corinthians 3:17 (AMB)

I realized how important it is to be born again. For many years, did not understand the meaning of being called Christian; I did not understand the meaning of this until now.

9 for He delivered us and saved us and called us with a holy calling [a calling that leads to a consecrated life—a life set apart—a life of purpose], not because of our works [or because of any personal merit—we could do nothing to earn this], but because of His own purpose and grace [His amazing, undeserved favor] which was granted to us in Christ Jesus before the world began [eternal ages ago], 10 but now [that extraordinary purpose and grace] has been fully disclosed and realized by us through the appearing of our Savior Christ Jesus who [through His incarnation and earthly ministry] abolished death [making it null and void] and brought life and immortality to light through the gospel, - (2 Timothy 1:9-10) AMB

Many times, I have heard the expressions born again, saved, and believer. - I did not know the meaning until I walked with Jesus Christ, the true living God, for more than ten years. - What does that mean? - Well, it means that if we have the Spirit of God within us, the natural spirit that we have from the moment we are born is superseded by the Spirit of the Lord.

7 then the Lord God [a]formed [that is, created the body of] man from the [b]dust of the ground, and breathed into his nostrils the breath of life; and the man became a living being [an individual complete in body and spirit]. (Genesis 2:7) AMB

That is where our old natural spirit comes from. - Now, the new Spirit that Jesus Christ places in us is called the Holy Spirit, Spirit of Truth, or Advocate, among other names, and it dwells in our being.

Everything within us is renewed, and we begin again as fresh new people while we are alive. It is like a spiritual transplant or transformation that we receive from the Lord, to replace the old man within us by putting the new man within us into a new being. - It is interesting and joyful to feel this feeling of splashing inside.

26 But the [a]Helper (Comforter, Advocate, Intercessor—Counselor, Strengthener, Standby), the Holy Spirit, whom the Father will send in My name [in My place, to represent Me and act on My behalf], He will teach you all things. And He will help you remember everything that

I have told you. 27 Peace I leave with you; My [perfect] peace I give to you; not as the world gives do I give to you. Do not let your heart be troubled, nor let it be afraid. [Let My perfect peace calm you in every circumstance and give you courage and strength for every challenge.] 28 You heard Me tell you, 'I am going away, and I am coming back to you.' If you [really] loved Me, you would have rejoiced, because I am going [back] to the Father, for [b]the Father is greater than I. (John 14:26–28) AMB

Let me better explain to you the meaning of being born again.

Again, Jesus answered:

3 Jesus answered Him, "I assure you and most solemnly say to you, unless a person is born again [reborn from above—spiritually transformed, renewed, sanctified], he cannot [ever] see and experience the kingdom of God." (John 3:3) AMB

Born Again—Spiritual Meaning: Beginning a new life in Christ means a new beginning, with a new teaching, new Spirit in you, new mind, new heart, new emotions, new thoughts, new feelings, new will, (new soul), new wisdom, new understanding, new intelligence, new transformation and a new renewal within you.

All of this becomes effective the moment you receive Jesus Christ as your Savior, and Lord in your heart; when you say the prayer of salvation out loud and have a humble heart that is willing to accept Jesus Christ, into your life. - As the Bible says, everything is new. - The old you (life-The previous moral and spiritual condition) are gone, and the new you (Spiritual awakening brings a new life) have begun. - From now on, we will not consider anyone from a worldly point of view.

16 So from now on we regard no one from a human point of view [according to worldly standards and values]. Though we have known Christ from a human point of view, now we no longer know Him in this way. 17 Therefore, if anyone is in Christ [that is, grafted in, joined to Him by faith in Him as Savior], he is a new creature [reborn and renewed by the Holy Spirit]; the old things [the previous moral and spiritual

condition] have passed away. Behold, new things have come [because spiritual awakening brings a new life]. (2 Corinthians 5:16–17) AMB

When you accept Jesus Christ as your Lord and Savior, the Holy Spirit (God) automatically begins to live within you, because Jesus Christ begins to live within your heart, and being; everything is renewed. Now, you have His mind, and you have His Spirit, His heart, and His righteousness, among others. - It is like freshwater gushing from a spring, gently touching you with a refreshing breeze, splashing into your being. - Is it not amazing? - This is what I call a miraculous life transformation: the mind, Spirit, and heart of the Lord, the true living God, begins to live within your heart.

He can communicate with you directly from Heaven, guiding you on the right path to follow here on earth. It is like starting to walk forward instead of backward, which is our natural, irrational way of walking. - Now, the Spirit and righteousness of God dwell in you. - Wow, super powerful! - Your consciousness or spiritual knowledge—ears, eyes, mind, mouth, and heart—takes place in your being, removing the veil in front of you and opening a new spiritual door of a new beginning in Jesus Christ. - Be wise and start a new life in the Lord! - Now, the second explanation of the meaning of being saved: If you declare with your mouth:

9 because if you acknowledge and confess with your mouth that Jesus is Lord [recognizing His power, authority, and majesty as God], and believe in your heart that God raised Him from the dead, you will be saved. 10 For with the heart a person believes [in Christ as Savior] resulting in his justification [that is, being made righteous—being freed of the guilt of sin and made acceptable to God]; and with the mouth he acknowledges and confesses [his faith openly], resulting in and confirming [his] salvation. 11 For the Scripture says, "Whoever believes in Him [whoever adheres to, trusts in, and relies on Him] will not be disappointed [in his expectations]." ... (Romans 10:9–11) AMB

Being Saved— Spiritual Meaning: Now, you are under the umbrella of the protection of Jesus Christ. - He will defend and protect you until the end of your earthly life, like a lion protecting its cubs. - You have two hundred and fifty angels available, protecting you all the time, as the Bible says. Also, your very being, your spirit, changes as a new person, yourself, or the other you, the first person within you, is born in the Spirit of the Lord. The way you think, and act is not the same as the way you used to act. - You live your life more in obedience because the Holy Spirit (the Spirit of God) guides you and shows you the way to follow, without compromising your free will. - It is like a switch that turns on inside you.

Consciousness and righteousness (soul) remain in alert mode all the time, and that helps you do what is rational, not the opposite. - If you do something contrary to God's will or find yourself in a dangerous situation, the Holy Spirit warns you immediately, telling your mind what to do, and the path to follow. - That way, you are not alone. It is up to you whether you listen or not. - The way you used to act, and think, was the irrational and natural way to respond to an action. - However, when you are saved, you learn to act in a rational, supernatural way, which is the opposite of the natural way. But the irrational and natural way you think changes completely within you to the supernatural.

9 If we [freely] admit that we have sinned and confess our sins, He is faithful and just [true to His own nature and promises] and will forgive our sins and cleanse us continually from all unrighteousness [our wrongdoing, everything not in conformity with His will and purpose]. (1 John 1:9). AMB

It is a supernatural restoration that only Jesus Christ, God, can do for us because He is our Creator, and it is a spiritual transformation. - The Spirit belongs to God.

7 then the dust [out of which God made man’s body] will return to the earth as it was, and the spirit will return to God who gave it. (Ecclesiastes 12:7) AMB

When we are saved, this guarantees our salvation. - That means we go to Heaven after our first death (when the flesh dies) because our Spirit is eternal and never dies. - Jesus seals and protects us, putting our name in the Book of life, so that when our flesh dies and we go to Heaven, the angels will know who we are.

That means that after we die (flesh), we do not go to hell but go directly to Heaven with the Lord, until the Second Coming of Jesus Christ, who promised to create a new Earth, a new Heaven, and a new life for everyone (Saved people).

25 Jesus said to her, "[a]I am the Resurrection and the Life. Whoever believes in (adheres to, trusts in, relies on) Me [as Savior] will live even if he dies; 26 and Everyone who lives and believes in Me [as Savior] will never die. Do you believe this?" - (John 11:25-26) AMB

We are guaranteed to live for eternity, from time to time, while we are alive and after death, until the time comes to live on earth again. - That will happen after the Second Coming of Jesus Christ. - We can live happily, young, and pleased to have the presence of the Lord with us all the time.

"24 "I assure you and most solemnly say to you, the person who hears My word [the one who heeds My message], and believes and trusts in Him who sent Me, has (possesses now) eternal life [that is, eternal life actually begins—the believer is transformed], and does not come into judgment and condemnation, but has passed [over] from death into life. (John 5:24) AMB

Salvation is especially important because it means that the spirit of darkness (Satan) no longer rules our lives or controls our thoughts, emotions, will, and feelings (Soul). - In this way, our behavior is directed on the right path. - Jesus paid a great price for us with His blood. - God came from Heaven to save us because he knew the Devil's plan and how easily he could deceive us, making us go the opposite way to the Lord. - The Devil has already been defeated by the Lord with His crucifixion, but since Jesus Christ was one hundred percent human and one hundred percent God (Divine), only His flesh was taken but not His Spirit.

That is why Satan is already defeated, and it is only a matter of time until the Second Coming of Jesus Christ, the true living God, to this earth again. - The Lord promised to make a new earth and a new Heaven for us. - Satan will no longer be there, and a new life will begin with only the presence of the Lord. Wow! - That is going to be phenomenal! Only good things will happen. - We will no longer know evil and vile. - Incredible promise! - The Lord is going to restore everything again. Salvation guaranteed us eternal life.

16 "For God so [greatly] loved and dearly prized the world, that He [even] gave His [One and] [a]only begotten Son, so that whoever believes and trusts in Him [as Savior] shall not perish but have eternal life. 17 For God did not send the Son into the world to judge and condemn the world [that is, to initiate the final judgment of the world], but that the world might be saved through Him. 18 Whoever believes and has decided to trust in Him [as personal Savior and Lord] is not judged [for this one, there is no judgment, no rejection, no condemnation]; but the one who does not believe [and has decided to reject Him as personal Savior and Lord] is judged already [that one has been convicted and sentenced], because [b]he has not believed and trusted in the name of the [One and] only begotten Son of God [the One who is truly unique, the only One of His kind, the One who alone can save him]. (John 3:16-18) AMB

Just as people are destined to die once, and then face judgment, so Christ was sacrificed once to take away the sins of many.

27 And just as it is appointed and destined for all men to die once and after this [comes certain] judgment, (Hebrews 9:27) AMB

10 For we [believers will be called to account and] must all appear before the [a]judgment seat of Christ, so that each one may be repaid for what has been done in the body, whether good or [b]bad [that is, each will be held responsible for his actions, purposes, goals, motives—the use or misuse of his time, opportunities and abilities]. - (2 Corinthians 5:10) AMB

17 Now the Lord is the Spirit, and where the Spirit of the Lord is, there is liberty [emancipation from bondage, true freedom] ... - (2 Corinthians 3:17) AMB

Now, the last and third explanation. Pay close attention; this is particularly important for a believer.

18 Jesus came up and said to them, "All authority (all power of absolute rule) in heaven and on earth has been given to Me. 19 Go therefore and make disciples of all the nations [help the people to learn of Me, believe in Me, and obey My words], baptizing them in the name of the Father and of the Son and of the Holy Spirit, 20 teaching them to observe everything that I have commanded you; and lo, I am with you always [remaining with you perpetually—regardless of circumstance, and on every occasion], even to the end of the age." (Matthew 28:18–20) AMB

Believer—Spiritual Meaning: Being a believer means believing and living the present life of the Old and New Testament in our lives, learning the complete words and language of Jesus Christ our God; believe that Jesus Christ died for us and saved us from sin (a path that leads us to destruction; spiritual or physical death). Believe that Jesus Christ is the Son of God and God. - The difference when a believer sin is that the Holy Spirit immediately prompts us and confronts us.

Once we understand, we repent and turn away from sin. - On the other hand, those unprotected or not saved by the Lord continue to sin, and never know it, because they see it as something normal in their lives, and they automatically distance Jesus from them. - So, they must go through difficult valleys for years and years, probably their entire lives, without understanding the truth about Satan, the father of lies (the spirit of darkness), or being delivered from the Lord.

When you read the scriptures and find the truth, the truth will set you free. - You believe that Jesus Christ is the Son of God and God, and you believe in all His promises. - Now, before you become a believer, you will need to see it, you will need to witness it and live it to believe it. - In over ten years of walking with the Lord, I have witnessed the transformation He has made in me, the protection I receive from the Lord and the angels every day, the loyal promises He has kept, and the miracles He has done in my life.

This allows me to give a full and confident response to my belief in the Lord as the true and only living God that exists. Furthermore, once we understand, experience and believe in His supernatural power within us, it allows us to walk with full authority. - So, we can call ourselves believers because Jesus Christ is not a religion, theory, theology, or philosophy. - He is the real and living God, and we now possess His Spirit, which enables us to do supernatural work for Him on earth, directly from Him in Heaven.

Jesus Christ is a Relational spirit; He is God, not a religion. Humanity created Him as a religion and made Him appear as such, but He is the true living God, who is relational within us; He is alive within us. - He is alive! - That is where the confusion comes from, and since people believe what others say without knowing it or experiencing it, that is where non-believers were born. God's not dead. - He is alive! - Our belief is not based on what we read or what other people tell us. Belief comes into effect when we experience and see His supernatural power working in us. Belief comes from the actions we experience, not from the books we read.

We become believers because we have witnessed His miracles in our lives and the transformation He made within us, as well as how He Blesses our lives and what He does in our lives. - It is an incredible experience, without a doubt! That is why we are called followers of Jesus Christ. - It is not a belief; It is a living action that we experience. - He also gave us full authority to teach or preach the Bible, baptize, cast out demons, perform miracles, heal the sick, and create disciples with the Holy Spirit.

17 These signs will accompany those who have believed: in My name, they will cast out demons, they will speak in new tongues; 18 they will pick up serpents, and if they drink anything deadly, it will not hurt them; they will lay hands on the sick, and they will get well." (Mark 16:17–18) AMB

Jesus Christ teaches us the invisible world (the spiritual world) and the lies of Satan so that we can help the visible world with the true Word of God. That is why it is called supernatural spiritual life; God is Spirit, and we, as His ambassadors (ministers) here on earth, become supernatural spiritual living creatures through His Spirit.

19 Listen carefully: I have given you authority [that you now possess] to tread on [a]serpents and scorpions, and [the ability to exercise authority] over all the power of the enemy (Satan); and nothing will [in any way] harm you. (Luke 10:19) AMB

We are the ambassadors of Jesus Christ on earth. - We are called to be the light of the world because when we show the fruit of the Spirit—Love, (which reaps) joy, happiness, goodness (the quality of being good), meekness (the fact or condition of being meek; submissive, humble), self-control, faithfulness, and kindness—we shine with God's principles, allowing us to keep the light of His heart burning within us. We are far from perfect, and we never will be, but living in Holiness (maintaining direct communication with God; the state of being Holy) is better than living without it.

22 "The eye is the lamp of the body; so, if your eye is clear [spiritually perceptive], your whole body will be full of light [benefiting from God's precepts]. (Matthew 6:22.) AMB

After returning from a coma in 2009, I noticed many changes in myself. One of the changes was that I had gained more knowledge, wisdom and understanding of things I did not know before. - I discovered that my spiritual being (relating to or affecting the human spirit or soul, as opposed to material or physical things) allowed me to identify my spirituality in Jesus Christ.

Christian Spirituality is the deepest thing within you: the quality of being concerned with the human spirit or soul, as opposed to material or physical things.

Let me explain the difference between being Spiritual and Christian Spirituality.

Being Spiritual is thinking, acting, and interacting from the consciousness of your own being (the deepest part of your spirit), since the spirit does not form the soul, nor can the body create. - Most of us are taught to believe that we are our physical forms, so we identify with our bodies or with the labels we give to our bodies, such as nationality, race, gender, or profession, among others. - This mistaken sense of self creates all the fear, anger, and sadness in our lives. - From a spiritual point of view, these emotions are always the result of the ego (misidentification), which then blocks access to your true spiritual nature towards the Lord, who is peaceful, loving, and joyful (see Evangelical Dictionary of Biblical Theology of Baker for more information).

Christian Spirituality is the knowledge of oneself as a spirit/soul and the understanding of one's highest spiritual qualities and attributes, which are love, peace, and purity.

Being Spiritual is the expression of these innate spiritual qualities through your thoughts, attitudes, and behaviors. - Being spiritual means that the ego has been dissolved, virtue has been restored to character, and spiritual values connect your inner being with the outside world (thoughts and actions). It is the ability to see all other human beings as soul/spirit and, therefore, transcend all false identities of race, color, gender, nationality, profession, and religion. It is in this awareness that we can recognize and connect with God.

Christian Spirituality is about Holiness (direct communication with God, Keep God in first place; Holy Spirit in you), which is the restoration of the human person to what he or she was created to be. - "Once you might say that Holiness involves the recovery of the integrity of our lives as they are being restored by the Spirit" (see Baker's Evangelical Dictionary of Biblical Theology for more information).

What is the Difference Between Being Spiritual and Christian Spirituality?

Christian Spirituality is knowing who you are in Christ and **Being Spiritual** is to realize who Christ is in you, and live life in that awareness.

You have always been who you are, and being in the truth, you can never be other than who you are, but it requires realization and awareness to understand the difference.

In that moment, when you see it, when you understand it, and then you feel it, that is when your spiritual life occurs. When we recognize and understand God for who He is, we develop a direct and dynamic relationship with Jesus Christ, the true living God. - It is the relationship that empowers us to bring out the core values of purity and love. - It is like children who experience the love, care, and protection of their parents; Only through that relationship can they understand it better. - Children who are not connected to their parents cannot experience these feelings, even if they have their own values. For me, I recognized and experienced my own inner beauty only when I came into a relationship with Jesus Christ. It is easy to have the knowledge and understanding of the self as a consenting being, but I was able to experience soul consciousness only because of my relationship with God.

For me, Christian Spirituality is not just a search for God, but I am spiritual, a practical embodiment of love and peace, only when I relate to God. - Therefore, it is not a search for God.

Christian Spirituality is when the search has ended, and the relationship has begun. I cannot connect with someone or have experiences or a direct relationship with them if I am still looking for them.

Christian Spirituality is charging the battery of the soul, but for that, I need to relate to God. - It is the only way to be a truly spiritual person, the only way! - Showing God's principles help us be better people in this world.

It is like when we are born for the first time. Since we do not have the justice of God, we walk backward. - We walk in disobedience because it is our nature, but when we are born again (receiving Christ in our hearts), that is when the justice of God takes place and comes upon us, causing us to walk forward, or walk in obedience. - After receiving Jesus Christ in my heart, my life changed completely.

The day I returned home from the hospital after coming out of the coma, I questioned myself, crying with a sharp, deep pain in my heart. "What am I going to do with my life, Lord? - Who am I, Jesus?" - I asked Him. - I was very sad to learn that I had to close my business and become permanently disabled.

I did not know which path to take at that moment or what to expect from my life. - I felt like I had nowhere to go. - I was trapped in the void of my thoughts and trapped in a body that did not belong to me because two weeks before, I had been someone else. - The desperation I had was inexplicable. - I was under major depression and did not give myself adequate time to heal my body, heart, and emotions, to even understand what was happening to me, at that time. - For many years, I lived in a world that did not belong to me.

I lived unhappily and was desperate to change for the better, but I did not know what to do, until that day when Jesus touched my forehead and my heart and changed me completely. - If I had to relive this experience repeatedly, I would live it with joy. - I would not change it for anything in this world because only God gave me the peace I never had. - Jesus gave me the understanding and love I was searching for many years. - Today, I have a purpose.

Today, I have a new beginning. - Today, I have the husband that God promised me a long time ago, and I am happy. I am incredibly happy to know that I am a new creature in Christ. - The old life is gone, and the new life has begun. - I have many dreams ahead of me, many goals that have been achieved today. - I am more than convinced that God has a purpose for my life, and I am here to fulfill it.

If you feel trapped in the emotions of your past, living an unhappy path in your present life, I advise you to seek Jesus Christ, the true living God. - Open your heart with acceptance to Him, pray the prayer of salvation, and receive Him, with all your heart, strength, soul, and love. You will be surprised how your life can change from one moment to the next, and you will live your life full of joy and love for Him. God is love, and that is what He is. God is Spirit, and if you allow Him to use your body as His temple, then He will be more than happy to dwell within you.

He wants to rescue your soul, which are your thoughts, emotions, will, and feelings that produce actions, and give you complete restoration in your soul with His love, through His Spirit, the Holy Spirit. - Do not miss the opportunity to meet Him and experience His magnificent love. - Trust me, you need it. - I need it.

We all need Him because before we were created as human beings, we were spirits, and He is our Creator. - I pray to the Lord that you realize that you are not alone. You are not abandoned. You have a Heavenly Father, who created you, and He is waiting for you to return to Him. He is not there to judge you or reject you.

He is there to hug you and say, "Welcome back, son or daughter. Welcome home!" I love you all with the love of the Lord. I hope this book can help you see God in a different way and help you restore your relationship with Him. Be Blessed in the name of the Lord.

Let us pray together,

Heavenly Father, I love You very much. Thank You for sending us Your Son, Jesus Christ, to die for our sins. Thanks to Him, I am a new creature in Christ. I ask for Your protection and guidance all the time. - I was very far from You all this time. Today, I want to start a new relationship with You. Please accept me into Your family and put my name in the Lamb's Book of Life. - I believe that You are the Son of God; You were resurrected on the third day, and today, you are seated at the right hand of the Heavenly Father. - I really want to start a relationship with You and honorably be called Your son or daughter, but it must be important; I need Your peace and love. - Please help me to be a better person and walk in obedience to please and honor You all the time. - In the name of Jesus, - I pray, Amen.

Chapter 6

Honoring Diego Pineda: A Mother's Guide to Processing the Loss of Her Son

36 Just as it is written and forever remains written,

"For Your sake, we are put to death all day long;

We are regarded as sheep for the slaughter." 37 Yet in all these things, we are more than conquerors and gain an overwhelming victory through Him who loved us [so much that He died for us]. 38 For I am convinced [and continue to be convinced—beyond any doubt] that neither death, nor life, nor angels, nor principalities, nor things present and threatening, nor things to come, nor powers, 39 nor height, nor depth, nor any other created thing, will be able to separate us from the [unlimited] love of God, which is in Christ Jesus our Lord.

- (Romans 8:36-39) AMB

I remember on Thursday, May 24, 2023. When only my beloved son, Diego Alejandro Pineda, was talking to me; that day, we talked about your frustrations and God. I took the opportunity to explain to you about the Creator, who is your Heavenly Father, and you took it very much together; your eyes lit up as if the night had known that it would be the last time I would see you.

My son, you took my life with you, but I hold on to the rock that is Christ Jesus, who sustains me every morning at 4 A.M. when I pray and ask Him for much strength to move forward and learn to live without you.

That Thursday, there was something very remarkable in you that I could not understand; although you told me it is better not to be alive, I could not understand your intentions, nor the speed you were going to do. It was 7 P.M. when I left for the house, and I remember that I told you Christ loves you! No, you told me nothing, but I know your heart rejoiced.

Years ago, in 2012, you and your brother Jose, who is with you in Heaven today, you and him were baptized, and thanks to you, I know Jesus today. I know that your greatest desire was to be with your brother, because you told me that Thursday when I went home, that day I thought that everything was still fine, the next day, I woke up very enthusiastic to know, that I had spoken to you about God, and that although you did not express it to me, your eyes lit up.

On Friday, May 25, - 2023, I was at a gas station with my husband Bruno, it was a sunny day but very strange, apparently. Sarah, your sister called me half an hour before she went to look for you, and told me that she does not feel well. I asked her why. And, "she answered," Because I have been trying to communicate with Diego, and he has not answered me, the GPS tells me that he has been in the same location since yesterday at 12:00 A.M., and he has not moved, that worries me, a little mom, Sarah, responds!

I was at the gas station at 10 A.M. When Bruno received a call from Sarah, confirming Diego's death; he took his life in desperation. When I saw my husband on his knees, and on the ground shaking his head, saying: - NO? - NO? - NO? I knew immediately that Diego was no longer in this world. I lay desperately on the ground looking at the sky, asking Jesus Christ for an answer: Why my son Lord, why? Howling in the middle of the street like a crazy woman. Without a sense of notion, I could not understand what had happened. I asked God Why, Lord? - What happened to the protective angels that I entrusted to you for my son? I pray to you every day for the protection of my children. What happened, Lord? What happened?

It seemed that everything was spinning in the opposite direction in slow motion; a girl was talking to me, and I did not understand. Everything turned into the emptiness of a memory. It was as if the wind of the night had been blown away and had vanished without us noticing. We ran towards the house, I felt that my life was ending, since Diego was a very special son for me. Diego took a very pleasant place in my heart, and his hugs left traces that can never be forgotten.

A week later, we were able to cremate my son, since he took his own life with a weapon and was unrecognizable, so we decided to cremate him. Pastor Richard of - the church "The New Covenant of Rock Hill, South Carolina" extended a very generous hand and did us a very special service, that remained in the memory of the sad mark of my heart when I saw my son in a jar of ashes when they gave him to me, it was the most devastating thing one could feel.

I write these words with my heart in my hand, crying, and with a broken soul, I pray for any mom who has gone through something like this, I understand what it is like to lose a child, but two in four and a half years, it is something that no mother can understand, that is why if you are going through something like this, I want to present my story to you as an example and rubbish, at the same time tell you that if it had not been for Jesus Christ, I would not have been here giving my testimony. I tried to take my own life when Jose, my oldest son, died four years ago several times, but I believe God knows what he does. -

My little son, you touched the depths of my soul. Today, my world has become empty and I'm sailing in space. Thinking about that Thursday we spoke last time, that same day was the time of your departure, that last goodbye; even without knowing it, you touched the deepest part of my feelings and Spirit.

I love you for eternity. I know that you rest in the arms of your Heavenly Father, Jesus Christ, the same one who gave your life. Fly, fly, fly, my son, free yourself in the heights next to God, I know that you are free and happy, every day I ask God to let me see you in vision so that I know that you are with your brother Jose, But after so much prayer I was able to see you in a dream with your brother, that fills me with joy to know that you are gathered in joy and love.

A day without you, everything remains in space, crooked and without movement. Everything I touch is into you and did not come to that. I always had a very high expectation of you, my son.

I love you with all my heart, I thank God for letting me know you even outside for twenty years, which gave me a lot of happiness. You are a special being, and I know that the Heavens rejoice in your presence. Tell the Almighty, that I thank Him for rescuing me. For having forgiven us, but much more for salvation, a salvation that is never lost. Once you are sealed with the Holy Spirit, you are the property of Jesus Christ. It fills me with great joy to know that you are by the side of the creator and your brother, Jose Pineda.

I do not know what happened on Thursday... I do not know what happened... Everything became confused, but I could never get over this, today I find myself in a mental lagoon that does not let me live, but that also gives me peace, because it is shipwrecked in the waters, this was your farewell, we took the ashes and your ashes were shipwrecked, my son, we looked for a very nice park where you stayed, as you always liked nature where you could be comfortable and free. My son, I know you are going to feel very well.

When you were a little kid, toddler, and adult, I was able to see how smart you are. Today, I only understand that only the Lord gave me your presence for twenty years. When I was eight years old, I was always terrified to know what was going to happen in 2020. Believe me that, for me, it is very difficult to say, but in 2019, my son Jose Pineda died, and at age twenty - my little boy, you took your own life, we do not know what happened, why, or the reason for the result.

Very sad to know that another good soul who suffered from "borderline personality disorder" and law that houses eight out of ten commit suicide. It is a very severe mental illness that parents should lend to their children, please do not abandon your children, including an uncertain ending, in my case the ending is very sad.... To know that you left me with a deep pain in my soul. I love you my son, I only ask Jesus Christ to keep you present before you, and finally discover who your Heavenly Father, Jesus Christ, is.

My heart is full of pain, Jesus Christ sustains me, He is my refuge in difficult times. Son, letting you go, was the saddest thing I have been able to experience. Today, I understand everything because the Lord has revealed it to me, I know it was an accident. I love you, my son, with all my heart. You are the most beautiful thing that has happened to me, I never thought that the end of this book could be dedicated to you.

Thursday is fading, I have asked the Lord to help me erase all this nightmare that I have lived with you, and your sad end, I do not know what happened to you, I do not know what was happening, all I know that you are, and will always be my son, until I came to meet with all of you. Lord, I ask you for strength to continue, because I feel sad, and so does the Holy Spirit. We are grieving.

Losing a child is a pain that no parent should ever have to endure. The loss of my son, Diego Pineda, has left a hole in my heart that can never be filled. As I navigate through the grief and try to find a way to honor his memory, I have turned to spiritual healing and the support of my loved ones.

Diego was a bright and talented young man with a smile that could light up a room. He had a passion for life and a kind heart that touched everyone he met. His sudden and unexpected passing has left me reeling, struggling to come to terms with the fact that he is no longer here with us. During my grief, I have found solace in honoring Diego's memory. I have created a space in our home dedicated to him, filled with photos, mementos, and reminders of the love and joy he brought into our lives.

I have also found comfort in seeking out spiritual healing. I have turned to prayer, meditation, and reflection to help me process my emotions and find a sense of peace. I have found strength in my faith, knowing that Diego is now in a better place and watching over me from above.

As I navigate through this difficult time, I have also leaned on the support of my family and friends. Their love and understanding have been a lifeline for me, helping me to cope with the overwhelming grief and find moments of joy amidst the pain.

Losing a child is a pain that no parent should ever have to endure. But through honoring Diego's memory, seeking spiritual healing, and leaning on the support of loved ones, I am finding a way to navigate through the darkness and find moments of light. Diego will always hold a special place in my heart.

In the end, the loss of my son has taught me the importance of cherishing every moment we have with our loved ones, and the power of love to heal even the deepest wounds. Diego may be gone, but his spirit lives on in the hearts of all who knew and loved him. And for that, I am eternally grateful.

Let us pray together,

Heavenly Father, I love You very much. Thank You for Your love and understanding, Thank You for having given me the children You gave me and the daughter I have; I ask You to strengthen and help me in my need, I ask You to guide me and enlighten my steps. May You restore my spirit, and my soul, from all the pain I endured. Thank You for your son, Jesus Christ, who fills me every day, and for The Holy Spirit, who never abandons me. Help me to be courageous and to seek more of You, - In the name of Jesus - I pray, Amen.

Chapter 7

Embracing the Unexpected: A Journey of Transformation

*"Life flows like a river, with unexpected turns.
Sometimes good, sometimes bad. Learn to enjoy
each turn because all these turns never come back".*

And do not be conformed to this world [any longer with its superficial values and customs], but be transformed and progressively changed [as you mature spiritually] by the renewing of your mind [focusing on godly values and ethical attitudes], so that you may prove [for yourselves] what the will of God is, that which is good and acceptable and perfect [in His plan and purpose for you].

Romans 12:2 (AMP)

Accepting the unexpected: a Journey of Transformation

Life is full of surprises, twists, and turns that we never see coming. At times, these unexpected events can be challenging and difficult to handle, but they can also lead to profound transformation and growth. Embracing the unexpected can be a powerful catalyst for spiritual healing and personal development. When we are faced with unexpected challenges or changes, it can be easy to resist and fight against them. We may feel scared, overwhelmed, or unsure of how to move forward. However, by accepting the unexpected and surrendering to the flow of life, we open ourselves to new possibilities and opportunities for growth.

Accepting the unexpected is not always easy, but it can lead to profound transformation and spiritual healing. When we let go of our need to control every aspect of our lives and trust in Jesus Christ, we allow miracles to happen. We can discover hidden strengths and talents within ourselves that we never knew existed, or we can find new paths and directions that lead us to greater fulfillment and happiness.

The process of accepting the unexpected is very personal and can be different for each person. For some people, it may mean letting go of past wounds and trauma, while for others, it may mean stepping out of their comfort zone and taking risks. Whatever form it comes in, accepting the unexpected requires courage, faith, and the willingness to surrender to the Lord, Jesus Christ, God.

As we navigate the twists and turns of life, we may encounter moments of doubt, fear, and uncertainty. However, by accepting the unexpected and trusting the process of transformation, we can find peace, clarity, and a sense of purpose. We may discover that the challenges we face are opportunities for growth and learning and that the unexpected events presented to us are gifts in disguise.

In the end, accepting the unexpected is a process of self-discovery and transformation. It is a path that leads us to a deeper understanding of ourselves and the world around us, and that can ultimately lead us to greater peace, joy, and fulfillment. When we learn to embrace life's unpredictability, we unlock a powerful approach to personal growth and resilience.

This journey of acceptance begins with a fundamental shift in perspective. Instead of viewing unexpected events as obstacles or disruptions, we can choose to see them as opportunities for learning and personal evolution. Each unexpected moment carries within it the potential for profound insight, challenging our preconceived notions and expanding the boundaries of our comfort zone. It is through these unplanned experiences that we often discover our true strength, creativity, and capacity for adaptation.

Embracing the unexpected requires a delicate balance of surrender and active engagement. It demands that we cultivate a sense of inner flexibility, allowing ourselves to bend without breaking when life takes an unanticipated turn. This approach doesn't mean passive acceptance, but rather a conscious choice to remain open, curious, and responsive to new circumstances. We learn to trust in our own ability to navigate uncertainty, recognizing that our resilience is far more powerful than any single unexpected event.

Moreover, this process of acceptance is deeply transformative. It teaches us humility, patience, and the art of letting go. We begin to understand that control is often an illusion, and true wisdom lies in our ability to flow with life's currents rather than constantly fighting against them. Each unexpected challenge becomes a teacher, offering lessons in emotional intelligence, self-compassion, and personal growth.

The beauty of accepting the unexpected lies in its potential for personal liberation. When we release our grip on rigid expectations, we open ourselves to a world of possibilities previously unseen. We become more present, more authentic, and more deeply connected to the rich tapestry of human experience. Our relationships deepen, our creativity flourishes, and we develop a more nuanced understanding of ourselves and others.

So, the next time life throws you a curveball, remember to embrace the unexpected and trust in the transformative journey that awaits you. Approach each surprising moment with an open heart and a curious mind. See each unexpected twist not as a disruption, but as an invitation to grow, to learn, and to discover the incredible resilience that resides within you. In doing so, you'll find that the most beautiful chapters of your life are often the ones you never saw coming.

> Approach each surprising moment with an open heart and a curious mind. See each unexpected twist not as a disruption, but as an invitation to grow, to learn, and to discover the incredible resilience that resides within you.

Let us pray together,

Heavenly God, I love You very much. Thank You for sending us Your Son, Jesus Christ, to die for our sins. Thanks to Him, I am a new creature in Christ. I ask for Your protection and guidance all the time. - Thank You for the restoration and healing I received every day. Help me to continue discovering new things in You, day by day, help me with my healing process, and transform me into a new creature in Christ. - In the name of Jesus, - I pray, Amen.

Chapter 8

Healing after Loss: The Story of Losing my Sons: Jose and Diego Pineda

Then He said to her, "Daughter, your faith [your personal trust and confidence in Me] has restored you to health; go in peace and be [permanently] healed from your suffering."

Mark 5:34 (AMP)

After the torment came the Restoration, after five years of agony, I was able to understand the excruciating pain that the loss of my two children could leave. It was not easy to rescue my soul from the deep pain that this left me. Only Jesus Christ, the true living God, could achieve it after much supplication and veneration.

Today, I feel calmer and happier, today, I enjoy total peace, and a new breath. In my being, today, I can say that I am free from so much agony that my soul felt. That is why, if you are going through something like this. I advise you to turn your eyes towards Jesus, He will be able to do what you and I will not be able to do; Restore our soul, there is no doubt, that if we walk with the power, and love of the Lord, Jesus. Everything will be easier on our path, but if we do not opt for His help perhaps; He will never be able to heal your spirit or soul.

In my life journey, I have experienced many traumas.

The trauma of my childhood left me with irreversible damage, at the same time, the loss of my dad. These last two traumas of my children were the bottom that I touched in my spiritual life. I also must thank the Lord for letting me live with them because today, I can communicate with you and offer you a helping hand for your spiritual restoration. Jesus Christ is the spiritually restored one, since He enters, into your soul and spirit and renews it again; I can only be a guide, and counselor, so that you go to Him.

I prayed to the Lord, that all those who have gone through a similar experience, will be restored by Him, and, above all, be touched by His Holy Spirit. Because without His Spirit, we cannot have the strength, or fortitude necessary, to follow the path of life.

The advice I want to give you today is to look for Jesus Christ of Nazareth. - He is waiting for you, and is ready to listen to your situation, whatever it may be. Never leave Him out of your plans because if you do, you will not be able to experience His Spiritual Favor. Keep going, a fall is not the end of your path, a fall is the beginning of a new learning, it is the beginning of a new stage in your path, and above all, it helps you realize what you are doing wrong. So, it is favorable to fall from time to time so that your conscience realizes that you are in the comfort zone, and you must change the course of the path.

The advice I want to give you today is to look for Jesus Christ of Nazareth. - He is waiting for you, and is ready to listen to your situation, whatever it may be. Never leave Him out of your plans because if you do, you will not be able to experience His Spiritual Favor.

When a loved one leaves you, and goes with the, Lord, to Heaven, they leave you with a deep spiritual pain, a pain that is difficult to explain, a pain that many cannot overcome, but by walking with Jesus, we come to understand the meaning; Coming to the conclusion of understanding the adversities that are also necessary for our journey.

I encourage you not to give up on the path of life because it is bright and pleasant, there is much to learn and unlearn; because our ancestors taught us what they learned, but in reality, it was not convenient in our lives in another way, that is achieved only when you come to the Presence of God, He will let you know what you should do.

God loves you; He loves you more than you can imagine, because God is love, and His love is Unconditional. Do not stop looking for Him, He is there by your side, if you do not see Him, it is because He is Spirit, and we cannot see Him, but we can feel Him and hear Him. Listen to Him as He whispers in your ear, and you will see great things in your life, achieving spiritual healing through Him.

Part Number Three
Scene Three: Why Should We Forgive?

Chapter 9

Forgiveness and Reconciliation: Two Paths to Inner Peace and Harmony to Our Relationship

15 But if you do not forgive others [nurturing your hurt and anger with the result that it interferes with your relationship with God], then your Father will not forgive your trespasses.

—Matthew 6:15 (AMB)

18 But all these things are from God, who reconciled us to Himself through Christ [making us acceptable to Him] and gave us the ministry of reconciliation [so that by our example we might bring others to Him],
19 that is, that God was in Christ reconciling the world to Himself, not counting people's sins against them [but canceling them]. And He has committed to us the message of reconciliation [that is, restoration to favor with God].

—2 Corinthians 5:18–19 (AMB)

After having a difficult childhood, and being sexually molested, my heart was empty and full of sadness. I realized that we cannot forgive, if we do not fully understand the reason for our behavior.

When we cannot forgive someone, ninety-five percent of the time, it is, because we are angry about our past. - The anger we show on the surface now is just a reflection of the pent-up anger we built up over the years. - Anger begins in our childhood. - We hurt ourselves spiritually without knowing why. - We become discouraged and ultimately heartbroken by all the unfair situations we have experienced in the past, or in our present lives. We do not understand the reason at that moment, because forgiveness opens a new door of understanding, to accept and deeply understand the circumstances we have experienced. - If you do not forgive, this door will not open for you.

We cannot move forward if we do not forgive the past. - We cannot move forward if we do not forgive ourselves and others. - Let me give you four steps that will help you forgive any circumstance you have had in your life. - Follow along and see the difference.

Step One: Identify the root of the Problem. Most of the time, you are angry about your past, and sometimes about our present. - Whether you were sexually abused, abandoned by your parents, divorced, lost a child, or suffered any other traumatic situation, you need to identify the spiritual pain that caused you to suffer the deepest pain in your heart.

** Identify the root of the problem/ Give one example here:*

Step Two: Write down your feelings. As soon as you discover the root of the problem, take some valuable time to express yourself on a piece of paper. - This exercise will help you clearly understand the main problem rooted in your heart, and better magnify the situation.

** Write down your feelings/ Express yourself here:*

Ask yourself questions, for example:

- When did I first suffer spiritual pain?

- How old was I?

- How did this happen?

- Who was my attacker?

- What was my reaction?

Ask whatever questions your Spirit tells you to write down, allowing the Holy Spirit to navigate through your thoughts, feelings, and emotions.

Then, give a humble and honest answer. - At this point, you may feel angry about that circumstance, but do not worry! - Just express yourself in the best way possible. - You will be surprised how much you will write. - Do not read this writing until two days later, or until you are ready to read it. - Before reading it and facing the great giant, you must first pray.

Ask Jesus for revelation, understanding, compassion, and wisdom, to accept what you could not change. - You will find out the truth in the end. - You will discover that you were only a victim of the circumstances you were experiencing at that time. - Nothing that happened was your fault. You realized that you are an innocent person with no knowledge or experience. - Do not worry about that; just let it out. - You will probably have a major spiritual breakdown that will leave you feeling heartbroken, but do not worry. This is part of the process.

The main point of this is for the Lord to cleanse and restore your broken heart.

Start talking to the Lord, expressing how you feel. - Cry, if necessary, and tell the Lord everything you feel at that moment. Then ask Him to forgive you, and restore your heart, to give you His peace. You will feel a supernatural movement moving towards you, and soon, you will be free of those memories that have tormented your heart for years, and that have contaminated your soul. - Your soul will be out of spiritual prison in no time. You will experience a magnificent, peaceful, and joyful feeling after this.

Now, a spiritual transformation will take place in your life.

Step Three: Forgive yourself. It is difficult to forgive yourself, because you discovered that you were a victim of circumstances that you did not choose to live in. Here, you need to clearly open your mind and understand this concept. - Stop for a second and think deeply. - Tell yourself that you are no longer a victim. - You are a conqueror in Jesus Christ, who strengthens you.

Why a winner?

Think about it: if you have come this far in life, it is because God has a purpose for you.

Furthermore, if you are still here, that means that the Lord has already declared you a victorious person in Him, simply because you endured so much spiritual pain in life and became triumphant in His presence. - You are here for a reason, do not forget it! - Not everyone has the strength to go far in life. - Trust me; Life is not that easy to handle, so you are more than a conqueror in Christ right now.

- Please do yourself a favor and forgive yourself. Send a letter to yourself, forgiving your past or present circumstances, forgiving all bad situations, as well as any unwanted moments that have happened, or bad memories you have. Read it aloud, embracing the forgiveness the Lord has given you. - God loves us so much and wants to forgive us, and give us His peace, the peace that the world cannot give.

27 Peace I leave with you; My [perfect] peace I give to you; not as the world gives do I give to you. Do not let your heart be troubled, nor let it be afraid. [Let My perfect peace calm you in every circumstance and give you courage and strength for every challenge.] (John 14:27) AMB

Make up your mind today! - Free your soul from the spiritual prison in which you find yourself. Be free and free others. Make the wise decision today to walk with a purpose: the purpose of forgiving yourself first. - You cannot forgive your past or others if you do not forgive yourself first. - You cannot move on unless you first forgive yourself and then others.

You cannot move on unless you first forgive yourself and then others.

Now, if you have forgiven yourself, embrace the victory! Be proud of yourself for having the courage to face the great giant of your life: all the unwanted feelings that you carried for years in your heart, (sadness, resentment, unhappiness, anxiety, condemnation, depression, and negative feelings), your memories that they were tormenting you. - That is now gone! - Hallelujah! Praise the Lord!

Only stable peace will remain in your heart. Live your life full of joy and peace. - Life is too short to live inside (heart) a spiritual prison of the past. The Spirit of the Lord is now in you. - Enjoy life to the fullest.

Rejoice in the Lord with the new transformation and Blessings that are about to come your way.

Remember that The Best is Yet to Come! Now, the Lord will pay you double for every problem you had, double joy, double peace, double love, double Blessing.

Step Four: Forgive Your Past and Others. This step is especially important, because your happiness (spiritual freedom) depends on this decision to forgive others. - Every time you forgive someone; you free yourself from any unwanted (negative) feelings. When you do not forgive others, it is like "drinking poison; waiting for the other person to die. Without realizing that the one who is dying is you.". - God is love and is quick to forgive. - We must follow that example to exercise forgiveness in our lives.

** Forgive yourself: Tell yourself that you are no longer a victim. - You are a conqueror in Jesus Christ, who strengthens you. Send a letter to you. Express yourself here.*

Jesus Christ constantly instructed us in the Bible to forgive and love others.

Why?

Because God is love, and if we absolutely love someone (ourselves and others), we must forgive their offenses as The Heavenly Father forgave us. - We need to deeply understand that we are human beings. - We are imperfect people, and we make many mistakes. - I bet when you were little, your parents did not want you to go through difficult times, but unfortunately, sometimes situations get out of hand, and things happen.

When I was little, I lived my life in my heart full of fear, terror, and anguish. - I did not know how to tell my parents about the sexual abuse I was experiencing at the time. - My dad was a violent person, and to be honest, I was afraid to tell my parents about that abuse, because I did not know what my dad's reaction would be towards me. - When I turned thirteen, I was already a person full of resentment and anger. - I did not know how to control myself or even express my emotions.

It was something I did not plan to feel; it just happened. - At that time, I was already captured in a spiritual prison, and my actions were irrational, because my soul was corrupted. When my first son, Jose, was born, I was incredibly happy, and I promised myself to protect my children from any of the unfair situations that happened to me in the past. - I did not want them to have the same experiences I had because it was very painful, spiritually and emotionally.

Unfortunately, I failed, because even though they were well protected, I was an angry person, and I could not be a better person for them. - I was doing what my dad did to us, in some way, for thirteen years, I did not know this was part of my trauma. - I thought this was normal behavior, until Jesus came into my life, and I discovered the truth.

8 'You shall not make for yourself an idol [as an object to worship], or any likeness (form, manifestation) of what is in heaven above or on the earth beneath or in the water under the earth. 9 You shall not worship them or serve them; for I, the Lord your God, am a [a]jealous (impassioned) God [demanding what is rightfully and uniquely mine], visiting (avenging) the iniquity (sin, guilt) of the fathers on the children [that is, calling the children to account for the sins of their fathers], to the third and the fourth generations of those who hate Me, 10 but [b]showing graciousness and lovingkindness to thousands [of generations] of those who love Me and keep My commandments. "Deuteronomy 5:8–10." AMB

The Bible tells us that sin and idolatry—idolatry can be a form of behavior, the shape of a figure, or simply putting anything first before God—giving first place, time, or importance to something before God.

Now, from the sin of our parents, we can inherit their behavior, conduct, or even their character, (that is a type of idolatry) can be punished by the Lord, from generation to generation, until the fourth generation, unless someone learns to love Jesus Christ, and begin a new life in Him, applying His principles and commandments in life. Then Jesus will forgive the sin. - That means that, for some reason, I emulated my dad's angry behavior toward my family (idolatry), until the Lord came into my life and freed me from the spirit of anger, rectifying my behavior toward my children and family.

Thank You, Jesus, for saving me. - I grew up in an angry home because of my dad and initially I brought that anger into my own home without realizing it. - I realized that when I gave my life to Jesus Christ. - When Jesus came into my life at age thirty-two, He changed me completely. - He took away the anger, the bitterness, the sadness, and the great weight that I had been carrying in my heart for years. - He helped me forgive those who hurt me the most, and He gave me His peace and His love, to the point that I no longer remember what they did to me.

Do yourself a big favor and forgive yourself and others intentionally. - Do not leave the rest of your life with this great weight on your heart. Do not allow your soul, and heart, to be condemned, feeling guilty for the past that you could not change. - Just because someone has not done right by you, does not mean you should live in a spiritual prison for the rest of your life. Go out! - Just forgive them, forgive them, forgive them for fun.

You would not regret it! - Make peace with your past, live your present happily, and plan your future, which is the difference you make today. Ask God to help you with this. He is the only one who can help you. - I was in psychological treatment for years, trying to understand why I felt this way. Do not get me wrong; The therapies helped me a lot, but they could not cleanse my soul and heart until Jesus Christ touched my heart.

He not only entered my heart, cleansing all the resentment I had, but he gave me a peace and love I had never felt before. Forgiveness is not something you just feel; It is a purpose in the action you take. It is a decision you make! - Do not let the Devil steal your peace and happiness anymore! - Decide to change, and you will see how Jesus works in your favor. - He will give you more than you could ever think.

Let's look at the following explanation about forgiveness, reconciliation, and the difference between the two.

Forgiveness—Spiritual Meaning: Forgiveness is an important action in our hands, to let go of the resentment, or anger we feel for the wrongdoings of others. The people in our lives often do something we do not like or approve of.

If these people turn out to be our friends or relatives, we become filled with bitterness towards them. - Most of us continue to hold grudges against our sinners for years and years. - Jesus said to hate sin; love sinners.

43 "You have heard that it was said, 'You shall love your neighbor (fellow man) and hate your enemy.' 44 But I say to you, [a]love [that is, unselfishly seek the best or higher good for] your enemies and pray for those who persecute you, 45 so that you may [show yourselves to] be the children of your Father who is in heaven; for He makes His sun rise on those who are evil and on those who are good, and make the rain fall on the righteous [those who are morally upright] and the unrighteous [the unrepentant, those who oppose Him]. (Matthew 5:43–45) AMB

22 And have mercy on some, who are doubting; 23 save others, snatching them out of the fire; and on some have mercy but with fear, loathing even the clothing spotted and polluted by their shameless, immoral freedom. (Jude 1:22-23) AMB

However, this is not the right approach in life, as we will always be full of resentment, and we will even contemplate revenge against those who have hurt our feelings.

Instead, all religions and spiritual people in the world teach us to forgive our sinners, and get rid of all negative feelings, so that we can have a clean heart, and move forward in life. - If someone has cheated on you, it is natural to hate them and feel hurt by those actions, but you can choose to forgive them. - You will feel the difference as all your bitterness will disappear instantly and you will feel better. - Once you are ready to forgive, you will improve the chances of joy, peace, and a new light coming into your life (Heart: Jesus).

32 Be kind and helpful to one another, tender-hearted [compassionate, understanding], forgiving one another [readily and freely], just as God in Christ also forgave [a]you. "Ephesians 4:32." AMB

Let us keep one thing in mind: sin; the action contrary to what is right to do in the eyes of God. - That evil action hurt us so much, more than we'll ever be able to express. However, we must forgive the sinner, the aggressor. - We need to deeply understand why this person did that to us. - Process that information in your brain first, and then, let it pass through your heart. Most of the time, people do things, because that is all they have in their hearts. You cannot be a good person if you have bad seeds planted in your heart. - You cannot give what you do not have, so you cannot receive what they cannot give you.

Reconciliation—Spiritual Meaning: Reconciliation is forgiveness in action followed by behavior.

People often say that they have forgiven their sinners, and that may be true, but they continue to hold grudges against those who have been involved in evil against them. - This may sound natural, considering the pain victims feel in their hearts, but these victims must pay a high price, for holding grudges, and holding on to resentment. - It is when you cleanse your hearts, and minds, of all kinds of feelings and emotions towards sinners that you begin to feel better.

They automatically begin to free their hearts from the spiritual prison in which they have been trapped for years. - Forgiving in thought, but not in actions, is incomplete forgiveness. When a victim cannot bear to see a sinner in their life, how can they say they have forgiven the person they hold a grudge against? - Of course, reconciliation is more difficult than forgiveness, since it requires practicing what you say in words. It is easier to forgive a cheating spouse than to reconcile with them and accept them back into your life as if nothing had happened.

18 But all these things are from God, who reconciled us to Himself through Christ [making us acceptable to Him] and gave us the ministry of reconciliation [so that by our example we might bring others to Him],
19 that is, that God was in Christ reconciling the world to Himself, not counting people's sins against them [but canceling them]. And He has committed to us the message of reconciliation [that is, restoration to favor with God]. "2 Corinthians 5:18–19" AMB

Reconciliation is the other part of forgiveness, and is necessary in our lives, just as we need air to breathe. - When you forgive someone but do not reconcile, it is like burning coal in your hand. - Every time you see this person, all your emotions, thoughts, and feelings rise and fall, and you feel a rush of anger slowly burning inside you.

This is extremely dangerous for you; It can affect your central nervous system, and your heart. - In some cases, it can cause a heart attack instantly. When you forgive someone, make sure your reconciliation is there, too. - Let go of anger, resentment, hatred, and any spiritual pain you feel, and ask Jesus to help you forgive this person, the same way He forgave you, to the point that you do not remember the person no more; The Evil action that person did to you. That is an honest reconciliation that produces forgiveness.

Practice reconciliation; It helps you increase your joy, peace, love, understanding, and wisdom, among others, especially those that free you from bad feelings, and emotions, leaving you out of the spiritual prison, in which you found yourself.

What is the difference between forgiveness and reconciliation?

Forgiveness is stopping the feeling of resentment and anger against our sinners or wrongdoers, while reconciliation is embracing the sinners in our lives.

Reconciliation is forgiveness in action followed by behavior.

Reconciliation is more difficult than forgiveness. - It requires courage.

Reconciliation must be our goal, or objective, so that we can have peace within us.

Jesus Christ is the same and never allows the behavior of others to change Him.

We cannot give what we do not have. - We cannot have what we cannot give. - We cannot change what they did to us. - All we can do is recognize the situation and change it for the better.

Forgiveness is a decision we make, but you must act with purpose. - You need to declare with your heart, and your mouth, that today, you want to forgive the person who hurt you the most.

15 But if you do not forgive others [nurturing your hurt and anger with the result that it interferes with your relationship with God], then your Father will not forgive your trespasses. (Matthew 6:15) AMB

Let us pray together,

Heavenly Father, I love You, and I want to do what always pleases You. - Please come into my heart and help me forgive those who hurt me the most in the past. Help me to wisely understand why they hurt me so much. Open my heart, Lord. Open my spiritual eyes. - Forgiveness is one of the hardest things to offer, but I know it is the best I can do. - Help me to reconcile with them, as You did with me.

Father, please forgive me for carrying all those toxic feelings for many years in my heart. - I stopped living my life to focus on what I feel. - I want to change, and I want to receive Your peace and love. - Please help me change. - Help me be a better person. Give me the courage to take the first step and change my life forever. - In the name of Jesus, - I pray, Amen.

Chapter 10

Why Should We Forgive: Keys to a Full and Happy Life

26 [a][But if you do not forgive, neither will your Father in heaven forgive your transgressions."]

(Mark 11:26) AMB

Forgiveness is a powerful tool that can lead to a full and happy life. It is the act of letting go of anger, resentment, and bitterness, towards someone who has wronged us. While forgiveness may seem difficult, it is essential for our own well-being and spiritual growth.

One of the key reasons why we should forgive, is that it allows us to let go of negative emotions that can weigh us down. Holding onto anger and resentment can lead to stress, anxiety, and even physical health problems. By forgiving others, we free ourselves from these negative emotions and create space for love, and peace, to enter our lives.

Forgiveness also allows us to experience spiritual freedom. When we hold onto grudges, we are trapped in a cycle of negativity that can prevent us from living a fulfilling and purposeful life. By forgiving others, we release ourselves from this cycle and open ourselves up to new possibilities and opportunities.

Within forgiveness lies the power to heal relationships and restore peace. When we forgive someone who has wronged us, we are able to mend broken relationships and move forward with love and understanding. Forgiveness allows us to see humanity in others and to recognize that we are all imperfect beings who make mistakes.

Forgiveness is an integral aspect of leading a full and happy life. When we choose to forgive, we free ourselves from the burden of holding onto resentments and grudges by accepting the shortcomings and mistakes of others, we enable ourselves to move forward and focus on our own personal growth. Forgiving others allows us to cultivate empathy, and compassion, and it serves as a powerful reminder of our own fallibility. It is through forgiveness that we can truly experience inner peace, and nurture healthy relationships with ourselves, and others.

One of the key benefits of forgiveness is its positive impact on our emotional well-being. Holding onto anger and resentment can be incredibly draining, causing our mental and emotional states to suffer. By choosing forgiveness, we release negative emotions and create space for love, joy, and happiness to flourish. When we forgive, we let go of the past and embrace the present moment, allowing ourselves to live more fully and experience greater contentment in life.

Forgiveness is also essential for cultivating meaningful and fulfilling relationships. Holding grudges and refusing to forgive can create barriers and lead to a cycle of conflict and unhappiness. When we choose forgiveness, we open the door to understanding and reconciliation, making way for healthier, and more harmonious connections, with others. It is through forgiveness that we build trust, deepen bonds, and create a supportive network of individuals who uplift and inspire us. Collectively, forgiveness not only enriches our own lives but also has a ripple effect, positively influencing those around us.

Ultimately, forgiveness is a key to finding inner peace and happiness. When we forgive others, we release ourselves from the burden of carrying around anger, and resentment. We can live in the present moment and experience joy and gratitude for the Blessings in our lives.

In conclusion, forgiveness is a powerful tool that can lead to a full and happy life, representing a profound act of emotional and spiritual liberation that transcends mere conflict resolution. By letting go of negative emotions, experiencing spiritual freedom, healing relationships, and finding inner peace, we can live a life filled with love and joy, breaking the destructive cycles of anger, resentment, and pain that often keep us emotionally imprisoned. Forgiveness is not a sign of weakness, but an extraordinary demonstration of strength, requiring tremendous courage to release the burden of past hurts and choose healing over continued suffering.

It is a transformative process that not only impacts our relationships with others but fundamentally reshapes our internal landscape, freeing us from the toxic energy of bitterness and creating space for personal growth, compassion, and emotional resilience. This powerful practice goes beyond simply pardoning another's actions; it is a deeply personal journey of self-discovery, emotional maturation, and spiritual evolution that allows us to reclaim our own power and peace.

By choosing forgiveness, we break the chains of victimhood and recognize our own capacity for compassion, understanding, and emotional freedom. Let us embrace forgiveness as a key to unlocking the full potential of our lives, understanding that this choice is ultimately an act of self-love and personal empowerment. Forgiveness has the remarkable ability to transform pain into wisdom, resentment into compassion, and brokenness into wholeness, offering us a path to a more meaningful, connected, and spiritually rich existence where we are no longer defined by our wounds, but by our capacity to heal and grow. Let's forgive, the same as the Lord, Jesus Christ forgave us.

> Forgiveness has the remarkable ability to transform pain into wisdom, resentment into compassion, and brokenness into wholeness, offering us a path to a more meaningful, connected, and spiritually rich existence where we are no longer defined by our wounds, but by our capacity to heal and grow.

Conclusion

We are at the end of the first part of the story. - I hope you connect with this book and realize that God loves you and He wants the best for you. - I suffered and endured physical and spiritual pain and fears in my heart. - At some point, life was unfair to me, or so I thought. -

However, I thank God for allowing me to be part of this injustice, because of that, I am stronger and the person I am today. - We all must endure all kinds of pain in this life: injustice, deception, agony, fear, or even terror in our hearts. We all have our own stories to tell, but no matter how much we suffer, God is always there, waiting for us to turn our gaze to Him.

He wants to be the one to carry our pains and sorrows and help us walk the path of life. - I had many reasons to hate my life and the people who made me suffer, but I have chosen not to hate them because God tells us to forgive the circumstances and forgive the people who hurt us the most.

In return, He gave me His priceless peace and love. - I have forgiven my past, my circumstances, my dad, my attackers, and myself. - Jesus came into my life when I needed Him most, and that pleases me because He promised not to leave me alone or forsake me. That is the promise He has for you today: to not be afraid to face the situation you are facing right now. - It could be a divorce, sexual abuse, injustice, people rejecting you, or anything that hurts your feelings. - He has promised to be there in times of need.

Today, I can say that I am free. I am free from condemnation. - I am free from spiritual pain, and I am free from sadness, only because I forgave all the people and the circumstances that hurt me the most in the past.

Right now, I am at peace with myself. - I am at peace with my past. - I am at peace in my Spirit, and my soul has been restored by The Lord, Jesus Christ of Nazareth. - But the most important thing is that I am at peace with God. - No matter how much we try to reject Jesus from our lives, He will always be there for us. - Because He loves us, He created us, we are part of His creation and His purpose.

7 Therefore, since we have these [great and wonderful] promises, beloved, let us cleanse ourselves from everything that contaminates body and spirit, completing holiness [living a consecrated life—a life set apart for God's purpose] in the fear of God. (2 Corinthians 7:1) AMB

Then, I acknowledged my sin to you and did not cover up my iniquity. I said, Blessed [fortunate, prosperous, favored by God] is he whose transgression is forgiven, and whose sin is covered.2 Blessed is the man to whom the Lord does not impute wickedness, and in whose spirit, there is no deceit.3 When I kept silent about my sin, my body wasted away Through my groaning all day long. 4 For day and night Your hand [of displeasure] was heavy upon me; My [b]energy (vitality, strength) was drained away as with the burning heat of summer. 5 I acknowledged my sin to You, And I did not hide my wickedness; I said, "I will confess [all] my transgressions to the Lord"; And You forgave the guilt of my sin. Therefore, let everyone who is godly pray to You [for forgiveness] in a time when You [are near and] may be found; Surely when the great waters [of trial and distressing times] overflow, they will not reach [the spirit in] him. 7You are my hiding place; You, Lord, protect me from trouble; You surround me with songs and shouts of deliverance. 8 I will instruct you and teach you in the way you should go; I will counsel you [who are willing to learn] with My eye upon you. 9 Do not be like the horse or like the mule which has no understanding, whose trappings include bridle and rein to hold them in check, otherwise they will not come near you. 10 Many are the sorrows of the wicked, but he who trusts in and relies on the Lord shall be surrounded with compassion and loving kindness. 11Be glad in the Lord and rejoice, you righteous [who actively seek right standing with Him]; Shout for joy, all you upright in heart. (Psalm 32:1–11) AMB

When we hide sin (disobeying God or doing the opposite of God's will) or keep it secret in our hearts without telling anyone, without even asking the Lord to forgive our fault, we automatically punish ourselves. This makes us feel heavy in our soul, spirit, and body, causing us to feel tired and sick. - That is why it is so important to forgive others and then ask our Heavenly Father God in Heaven to forgive our sins. - The Bible says that life is a circle; everything revolves around it. What you give is what you receive.

If you forgive, God will forgive you. - You will automatically break out of the spiritual prison you have been in for years, and experience spiritual freedom in your inner being. - God is Spirit, not a religion. - Reestablish a relationship with the Spirit of the Lord today, so that you can live in full forgiveness and joy. Do not waste any more time; start today! - Call Jesus. - He is waiting for your return. Establish a spiritually intimate relationship with the Lord.

Trust me; You would not regret it!

Jesus has a Message for your Today

7 Beloved, let us [unselfishly] [a]love and seek the best for one another, for love is from God; and everyone who loves [others] is born of God and knows God [through personal experience].

(1 John 4:7) AMB

My beloved Sons and Daughters,

I want to tell you that I love you with all my heart, that my greatest desire is to give you eternal salvation. I know that you have gone through valleys of dry and rocky bones in life, but I have been there strengthening you, and helping you get out of them; although you do not see me, but I am always there, aware of what you do, watching you, and guiding you. I have never abandoned you, and I never will. Today is a very special day, because I can express these words of faith for you. Today a new chapter opens in your spiritual life, and I want you to know that I am attentive to your voice to listen to you to see what you need and want.

My Son., One day I created you with great care and devotion, I put seeds of greatness in your heart, so that you could develop and be what you always wanted to be, if today you have not been able to be what you have dreamed of, it is because you have not wanted it, or desired it; You have not fought hard enough for it. Despite your silence and absence, I always carry you in my heart and wish the best for you.

Son, I forgive you for all the faults you have done, for your absence, but above all, for not having met me before. But today, I open the doors of my heart to you, so that you can come to me, and we can begin a pure and honest relationship together. Today, I open the Heavenly doors in your favor, so that you understand how much I love you, and I offer you Salvation so that my Spirit may dwell in you, and you can enjoy my presence.

God loves you and always has, but you are the one who refuses to know Him, come to me, seek for me, I am Jesus Christ the Almighty, the creator of Heaven and Earth and everything there is in it. Do not be afraid, because I am your Heavenly Father, and through me, you were created with the spirit that gives your life. My son does not forget these words, because I am with you, and I am always ready for you to call me, and we can be friends.

Do not give up in the face of adversity, remember that there is always an opportunity to move forward and, above all, learn. Learn to forgive and let go, live in the present moment and stop worrying about the past or the future, practice gratitude and appreciate what you have, surround yourself with people who appreciate and care for you, always. Be kind, treat others as you would like to be treated; that is the essence of life. Do not compare yourself to others and accept your own uniqueness, spend time on activities that you like and that relax you. Learn to listen and communicate effectively, be aware of your thoughts and emotions, and learn to manage them.

Learn to say – "No" when necessary and set boundaries, practice empathy, and try to understand the point of view of others. Surround yourself with nature and enjoy the world around you, do not worry about the things you cannot control and focus on what you can, learn to enjoy silence, and the soul, be patient, and accept that, everything takes time.

I love you with all my heart, Jesus!

Quiet the Mind: Exploding Meditation and Reflection for Inner Peace

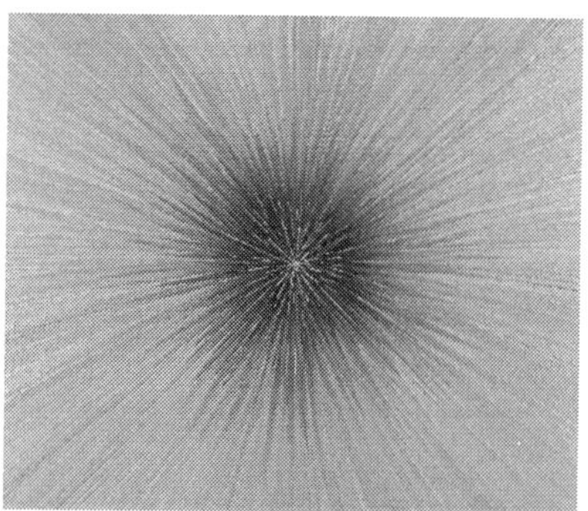

There was a mouse who was always distressed because he was afraid of a cat. - A magician felt sorry for the mouse and turned him into a cat. - Then he became afraid of a dog, so the magician turned him into a dog. Then, he was afraid of a panther, and the magician turned him into a panther. - Then he felt afraid of the hunter.

At this point, the magician gave up and turned him back into a mouse, telling him,

"Nothing I do for you will help you at all because you will always have the heart of a mouse." - Understand this: no matter how much we try to change our exterior; we will never be the person we are made to be.

“True change begins within us first. - In this way, our exterior can reflect the light of our heart. - Let's change our interior with positive affirmations and actions so that one day we can look like panthers while still being mice.”

Father, thank You for everything You have done for me. - I only have immense gratitude in my heart to offer You. - In these more than ten years that I have walked with You, I can see in my being that You have transformed me tremendously, making me a pure being, full of love. - My language has completely changed, and my thoughts have an overabundance of Your goodness. -

Today, I want to express the following affirmations:

I am a star with my own Light, because I am a creation of God. Prosperity comes to me effortlessly, because I am part of creation, and I deserve it. - I am Divine health manifested in my body, here and now.

Today, I am the happiest person in the world, because the Almighty lives in me. - God is the one who gives me power and makes my path perfect. - Today, I give thanks for everything I have received. I am smart, beautiful, and my body is healthy. - I give a lot of love. - I am important and valuable. - I am capable, and determined, to do everything I need to do. - I am a loving person and expect a lot from myself.

There is no obstacle that I cannot overcome because I am strong; Heaven conspires in my favor. - I feel happy, cheerful, and healthy, with abundant energy, and vitality to do everything I set my mind to, because I am a Divine energy. - I can do all things through Christ who strengthens me. - I have health and happiness. Jesus Christ grants me peace, love, and abundance. - I love everyone, because God is love, and He is dwelling in me.

Today is a wonderful day, because Jesus is in me. - I am powerful, happy, joyful, invincible, and I enjoy great abundance in my life, because the kingdom of God is in me. - I am deeply grateful for that. Thank You, Father, for allowing me to access all the opportunities that You bring my way. - I understand that the universe is infinite and inexhaustible.

With my thoughts I can achieve my dreams and goals, giving shape to the universal substance that we can all share with all the love in the world. - I am happy!

My life is full of love, health, peace, prosperity, and harmony. Every day is better than the last. - God has been generous to me, thank You! - I accept myself as I am and allow myself to think only in terms of abundance, love, gratitude, joy, and happiness. - Every day, I am better than ever, financially, spiritually, and healthy.

I have no words to express the deep love I feel for You, God. Lord, every day, I am more prosperous and joyful. - Life is the greatest opportunity you have given us. - Therefore, we learn how to be true human beings. Thank You, God, for such a beautiful opportunity. - I am the magnified energy that enters, flows, fills, and rejuvenates every cell of my body and mind, by eliminating everything that does not resemble it. - The Lord's infallible provision fills my mind and heart with love.

Thank You for all the abundance in this universe that I can enjoy, explore, and live. Today, I can enjoy money, love, and health. - I am happy in everything I wish to do, and I have accepted the presence of Your love that fills me, guides me, strengthens me, and inspires me. - I know that I can do everything with the favor of Your Spirit, because Your desires are one with me, in a harmonious, orderly way, and in due time I will achieve my intentions; which have their own power of organization. In my life, money flows easily. - I am attracting abundance, wealth, health, love, peace, and happiness.

Today is the best day that God has created, so I enjoy it and fill it with happiness to live it, even in times of confusion. - I learn from the good but more from the adversities of life. Thanks to them, I can train, learn, grow, mature, and understand to be a better human being. - I am well equipped and empowered because the Spirit of the Lord is in me and upon me.

17 Now the Lord is the Spirit, and where the Spirit of the Lord is, there is liberty [emancipation from bondage, true freedom]. 18 And we all, with unveiled faces, continually y seeing as in a mirror the glory of the Lord, are progressively being transformed into His image from [one degree of] glory to [even more] glory, which comes from the Lord, [who is] the Spirit. (2 Corinthians 3:17-18) AMB

I have everything I need, Father, because You already conceived it for me.

I am happy in everything I wish to do, and I have accepted the presence of Your love that fills me, guides me, strengthens me, and inspires me. -- I am deeply grateful to all the people who have shown me something, even in unpleasant or difficult times, because there is always something to learn. - I reflect, and I can learn, and I thank You for that opportunity. -

I believe that bad circumstances can always teach us something. - I learned something good from there; It is where our personal and spiritual development comes from. - I only focus on the good and learn from the bad, so there is always something good to learn. - I deeply appreciate this opportunity, which only makes me a better person. - If anyone offers me a word of encouragement, their time is greatly appreciated. If I can, I achieve it, I deserve it, I Bless it, and I am always prepared for more. I have abundance, love, and so much prosperity.

I work every day to get more so I can be a better person. - I have a job that I love, and I enjoy doing it with a lot of love, to all the people who have shown me something, even in unpleasant or difficult moments, because there is always something to learn. - I reflect, and I can learn, and I thank You for that opportunity. - I believe that bad circumstances can always teach us something.

I learned something good from there; It is where our personal and spiritual development comes from. - I only focus on the good and learn from the bad, so there is always something good to learn. - I deeply appreciate this opportunity, which only makes me a better person.

I have the job that I love, and I enjoy doing it, with a lot of love, harmony, sincerity, joy, and excellent health. - I walk with excellence for my Father, God; All power has been given to me.

I have enough time, energy, wisdom, and money to achieve all my goals and dreams. - life is beautiful, phenomenal, and excellent; it teaches us every day to be better people, whom I treasure and care for with great love.

I am a being of value to Jesus Christ, my Father, who formed me. I am perfect in my Spirit, and today. - He lives inside my being. - His Spirit strengthens me and puts, takes away, and modifies perfection in me. - I am a daughter of the Highest, for whom he walked with justice, love, peace, joy, happiness, and goodness; I have so much mercy for others. If I can create and give a smile, I am also capable of creating and receiving the destiny I want.

Today is a great day because You created it. I have all the positive energy to achieve my goals. - Thank You, Jesus! - I forgive and move on. I have a lot of abundance, health, and love around me. - I give what I want to receive, so I receive what I give. - I am happy. I am a being of Light and salt. Thank God for all the abundance. - I live in peace and joy, and I am in the process of achieving all my goals. - I am victorious, kind, gentle, delicate and I have self-control, but above all, I have a lot of love to give. - I am excellent, and for that, I have everything excellent.

I am deeply happy, and I know that I attract love, peace, prosperity. - I am a magnet that attracts only the positive. When I make a mistake with someone or something, I realize it at that moment, and quickly confront my mistakes. - I reconstruct my faults and apologize because I am a humble being. - If God is with me, nothing and no one can be against me. - I am the greatest treasure for God, that is why I take care of myself and love my life without becoming obsessed.

I love and forgive all those who offend me, because they are also human beings. - In my heart, there is only love, peace, patience, kindness, forgiveness, faithfulness, self-control, joy, health, happiness, and a lot of humanity.

Most of the time, we strive to change our exterior by leaving the other self, the inner self, outside. - Our spirit is the first being within each of us. We cannot abandon it and think that it is not important to feed it with spiritual words that come from the Word of God because, without our exterior, it will not be able to shine with its own light.

Your eyes reflect what is inside you, so look at them and discover if you live in the Light or the darkness. - If you are living in darkness, then it is the right time to turn around and ask our Savior and God, Jesus Christ, to indwell you. God told us in the Bible that in life, we will have afflictions, but if we are with Him, everything will be easier. -

Father, thank You for the change you are making in me every day. Thank You for Your unconditional love that has no end. - Thank you for the privilege of being alive. - Life is one of the greatest gifts you gave as a token of your love. Thank You for all the opportunities that present themselves every day. - Thank You for living within me through your Holy Spirit.

Thank You for the sacrifice of my sins. - Thank You for allowing me to have direct communication with You. - You always guide me and teach me. Thank You for the children and grandchildren you have given me. Thank You to my beautiful family, friends, and excellent people that you put in my life with so much value.

Thank You for never abandoning me in times of adversity. - Thank You for giving me the opportunity to have my sons, Jose and Diego, and allowing me to share such beautiful and unforgettable moments with them. Today, my soul rests in Holy peace, knowing that today they are by Your side, and that You take care of them. Because they are with you, I know they are in better hands. - Thank You for the renewed, alert, and receptive mind You gave me. - Thank You for all the wonderful words You say to me that only encourage and motivate me to keep going.

Keep in mind that thoughts are a habit, and like any other habit, you can change and master them whenever you want. - It just requires repetition. - Look in the mirror and say the following affirmations above. After you are done, you will experience a total transformation in your being.

Part Number Four
Salvation Demystified: The Key to Eternal Life and Redemption

Chapter 11

Jesus is Spirit

17 Now the Lord is the Spirit, and where the Spirit of the Lord is, there is liberty [emancipation from bondage, true freedom].

(2 Corinthians 3:17) AMB

Jesus is often referred to as the Son of God, the Savior, and the Messiah. But did you know that Jesus is also Spirit? In the Bible, Jesus is described as both fully human and fully Divine, which means that he is not limited to a physical body. Instead, Jesus is a Spiritual being who transcends the physical world.

One of the key aspects of Jesus being Spirit is His connection to the Holy Spirit. In the Christian faith, the Holy Spirit is the third person of the Trinity, alongside God the Father and Jesus the Son. The Holy Spirit is often described as the presence of God in the world, guiding and empowering believers to live out their faith. Jesus, being Spirit, is intimately connected to the Holy Spirit, working in harmony to bring about God's will on earth.

When we think of Jesus as Spirit, it can be easy to get caught up in theological debates and complex doctrines. But at its core, the idea of Jesus as Spirit is a comforting and reassuring one.

It means that Jesus is not limited by time or space, but is present with us always, guiding us and comforting us in our times of need.

So how can we connect with Jesus as Spirit in our daily lives? One way is through prayer and meditation. By quieting our minds and opening our hearts to the presence of Jesus, we can experience His Spirit in a profound and transformative way. We can also look for signs of Jesus' Spirit at work in the world around us, in acts of kindness, moments of beauty, and times of peace.

The concept of Jesus as a spiritual entity is deeply rooted in Christian theology. Central to this belief is the understanding of Jesus as the embodiment of the Holy Spirit. The Holy Spirit is seen as the Divine Presence of God, guiding and empowering believers to live a life aligned with God's will. In this perspective, Jesus is regarded as the perfect example of Holiness and compassion, imparting spiritual wisdom and transforming lives through His teachings and actions.

The belief in Jesus as the Holy Spirit is based on biblical teachings. The New Testament presents Jesus as the Son of God and part of the triune nature of the Divine, along with God the Father and the Holy Spirit. The Holy Spirit is often referred to as the Comforter, Advocate, or Helper, emphasizing the role of Jesus in guiding and empowering believers. This understanding affirms the transformative power of Jesus' life, death, and resurrection, as the Holy Spirit continues to be present and active in the lives of believers today.

Recognizing Jesus as Spirit goes beyond the idea of a historical figure or merely a spiritual leader. It invites individuals to experience a personal relationship with Jesus, understanding Him as a Spiritual power that can bring inner peace, healing, and salvation. Embracing Jesus as the Holy Spirit means embracing the teachings and values He embodied, such as love, forgiveness, and selflessness. By acknowledging Jesus as Spirit, individuals can tap into a source of Divine guidance and inspiration, leading to personal growth, Spiritual transformation, and a deeper connection with God and others.

In conclusion, Jesus is Spirit, a Divine being who transcends the physical world and is intimately connected to the Holy Spirit, embodying the profound mystery of spiritual existence beyond human comprehension. By recognizing Jesus as Spirit, we can deepen our faith and experience His presence in a powerful way that goes far beyond intellectual understanding, touching the very core of our spiritual being. This Divine essence is not confined by temporal or spatial limitations, but instead permeates the universe, offering a transformative connection that bridges the gap between the human and the Divine. The spiritual nature of Jesus represents a profound theological concept that invites believers to move beyond literal and materialistic interpretations of faith, encouraging a more intimate and personal relationship with the Divine.

This understanding challenges us to perceive spirituality not as a distant, abstract concept, but as a living, dynamic presence that can actively engage with our daily experiences, thoughts, and emotions. So let us open our hearts and minds to the Spirit of Jesus and allow Him to guide and comfort us in all aspects of our lives, recognizing that this spiritual connection has the power to provide healing, wisdom, and profound inner peace.

By surrendering to this spiritual presence, we can experience a transformative journey of faith that transcends human limitations, offers hope in times of struggle, and provides a deeper, more meaningful understanding of our existence and purpose. The Spirit of Jesus invites us to a holistic spiritual experience that encompasses not just our intellectual beliefs, but our entire being - mind, body, and soul.

Chapter 12

Who is Jesus?

63 But Jesus kept silent. And the high priest said to Him, "I call on You to swear a binding oath by the living God, that you tell us whether You are the Christ, the Son of God."

(Matthew 26:63) AMB

Have you ever pondered the question:

Who is Jesus Christ?

Jesus is not only the son of God, but He is also our Savior and is Divine in nature. God, by embracing His teachings and following His example, we can experience boundless peace and joy. This reflection of His love can be seen in our lives as we discover our true purpose.

Now, if Jesus Christ is God, then who is this God? God is a Spirit, specifically the Holy Spirit. It is through the Holy Spirit that Jesus Christ resides within our hearts, bringing us a refreshing and overflowing love. This Divine presence grants us peace, joy, and comfort, even during the most challenging moments. In essence, Jesus Christ, our Almighty God, dwells within us.

Jesus is not only the Son of God but was sent to Earth by our Heavenly Father to bear the sins of all people. This act of sacrifice and forgiveness was made possible because of Jesus' Divine nature and perfect life. He was more than just a teacher and servant; when asked by the apostle Peter who he truly was, Peter proclaimed Him as the Christ, the Son of the living God.

Jesus serves as the perfect example for us to follow. Through His flawless life, he showed us the path to reunite with our Heavenly Father. Despite never having sinned, Jesus was baptized to exemplify obedience to God and to teach us the importance of baptism for all believers.

To truly follow in His footsteps, one should consider being baptized in a Christian church. Love was at the core of Jesus' teachings and actions. His compassion extended to the poor, the blind, and even those who crucified Him. His love knows no bounds and is accessible to anyone in need.

Jesus' teachings encompassed various aspects of life, including the way we live and how we treat others. Even at the young age of twelve, He astounded scholars with His knowledge and became the greatest teacher of all time. Jesus conveyed important lessons through relatable stories or parables, which continue to inspire and motivate us in our journey to follow Him and serve others.

One cannot overlook the significance of Jesus' suffering and crucifixion, which He willingly endured to save us from our sins. His mission on Earth was to redeem humanity, and He paid the ultimate price for our mistakes. Out of immense love, Jesus suffered in the Garden of Gethsemane, carrying the weight of every sin and pain known to humanity. Despite the cruelty he faced, he showed mercy even to those who were responsible for His death.

Throughout our lives, we will inevitably make mistakes, but by striving to be better and seeking forgiveness from our Heavenly Father, we can cleanse our souls. We are forever indebted to the love and sacrifice of our Savior and Redeemer, Jesus Christ. Through Jesus Christ, we can find lasting peace. He is known as the Prince of Peace, and by embracing His teachings, we can experience true and eternal peace.

The resurrection of Jesus is a pivotal and triumphant event in history, representing the cornerstone of Christian faith and the ultimate demonstration of Divine power and love. Three days after His death on the cross, Jesus rose from the tomb and appeared to His friends and followers, transforming what seemed to be a moment of ultimate defeat into the most profound victory in human spiritual experience. He was the first to be resurrected, signifying the reunion of His spirit with His perfected physical body after death, a miraculous event that transcends human understanding and offers hope beyond the limitations of mortal existence.

This supernatural occurrence is not merely a historical event, but a powerful theological declaration that death is not the final destination for humanity. Through Jesus conquering death, we are assured that we, too, will be resurrected one day, with the promise of eternal life and reconciliation with God.

The resurrection represents more than a miraculous moment; it is a profound spiritual truth that speaks to the transformative power of faith, the redemptive nature of Divine grace, and the potential for spiritual renewal and regeneration. It symbolizes hope emerging from despair, life, conquering death, and the potential for spiritual transformation that exists within everyone who embraces this foundational Christian belief. The resurrection of Jesus offers believers a compelling narrative of redemption, demonstrating that suffering and death are not the end, but can be pathways to spiritual rebirth and ultimate triumph.

Chapter 13

Repentance: Key to Free Yourself from the Past and Live in Peace

19 So repent [change your inner self—your old way of thinking, regret past sins] and return [to God—seek His purpose for your life], so that your sins may be wiped away [blotted out, completely erased], so that times of refreshing may come from the presence of the Lord [restoring you like a cool wind on a hot day];

(Acts 3:19) AMB

Repentance is a powerful tool that can help you free yourself from the burdens of the past and live in peace and harmony. It is the act of acknowledging your mistakes, feeling remorse for them, and making a conscious effort to change your ways. By repenting for your past actions, you can release yourself from the guilt and shame that may be weighing you down and move forward with a clean slate.

One of the key benefits of repentance is that it allows you to let go of the past and start fresh. When you hold onto feelings of guilt and regret, it can be difficult to move forward and live in the present moment. By repenting for your past mistakes, you can release yourself from the negative emotions that are holding you back and create space for peace and happiness in your life.

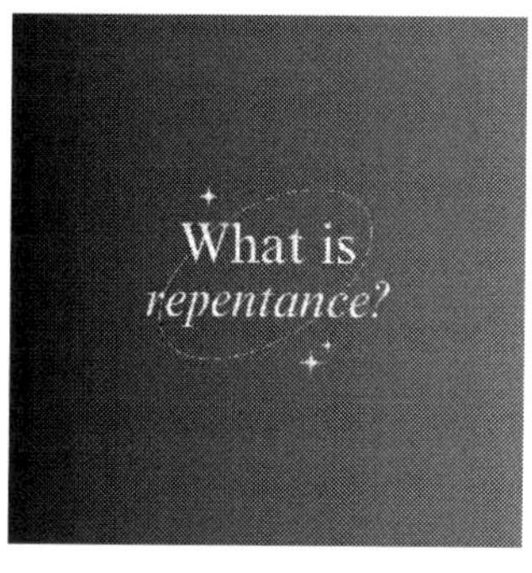

"The True change transformed from a conscience willing to change a wrong action"

Repentance also allows you to take responsibility for your actions and make amends for any harm you may have caused. By acknowledging your mistakes and seeking forgiveness from those you have wronged, you can begin to heal the wounds of the past and restore relationships that may have been damaged. This process can bring a sense of closure and resolution, allowing you to move forward with a clear conscience and a renewed sense of purpose.

Living in peace and harmony is essential for overall well-being and happiness. When you can free yourself from the burdens of the past through repentance, you can experience a greater sense of inner peace and contentment. By letting go of negative emotions and focusing on positive change, you can create a more harmonious and fulfilling life for yourself and those around you.

To truly free yourself from the past and live in peace, it is important to approach repentance with a relaxed and open mindset. Allow yourself to be vulnerable and honest about your mistakes and be willing to make amends, and seek forgiveness. Remember that everyone makes mistakes, and that true growth and healing come from acknowledging and learning from them.

By embracing repentance as a key tool for personal growth and transformation, you can free yourself from the burdens of the past and create a more peaceful and harmonious life for yourself and those around you. Take the time to reflect on your actions, seek forgiveness where needed, and commit to making positive changes moving forward. In doing so, you can release yourself from the chains of the past and step into a brighter, more peaceful future.

Chapter 14

The Danger of Ignorance: Find Out How a Lack of Knowledge Can Affect Your Life

My people are destroyed for lack of knowledge [of My law, where I reveal My will].

Because you [the priestly nation] have rejected knowledge,
I will also reject you from being My priest. Since you have forgotten the law of your God,

I will also forget your children.

(Hosea 4:6) AMB

Ignorance is not bliss. In fact, it can be quite dangerous. The danger of ignorance is real and can have a significant impact on your life. When you lack knowledge about a certain subject or situation, you are more likely to make mistakes, miss opportunities, and even put yourself in harm's way.

One of the biggest dangers of ignorance is that it can lead to poor decision-making. Without the necessary information, you may not be able to fully understand the consequences of your actions. This can result in making choices that are not in your best interest or that have negative repercussions. For example, if you are ignorant about the risks of a certain investment, you may end up losing a significant amount of money.

Ignorance can also prevent you from taking advantage of opportunities that come your way. If you are not knowledgeable about a particular industry or field, you may miss out on job opportunities, promotions, or chances to further your education. This can limit your potential for success and personal growth.

Furthermore, ignorance can also be a threat to your health and safety. If you are unaware of the dangers of certain substances or activities, you may unknowingly put yourself at risk of harm. For example, if you are ignorant about the effects of smoking, you may continue to engage in this harmful habit without realizing the long-term consequences it can have on your health.

To avoid the danger of ignorance, it is important to actively seek out knowledge and information. This can be done through reading, research, asking questions, and seeking out experts in the field. By educating yourself, you can make more informed decisions, seize opportunities, and protect yourself from potential harm.

The danger of ignorance lies in its potential to negatively impact various aspects of one's life. A lack of knowledge can hinder personal growth and limit opportunities for success. Without a solid understanding of the world around us, we become vulnerable to manipulation and misinformation. Ignorance can lead to poor decision-making, which can have long-lasting consequences on our careers, relationships, salvation, and overall well-being.

The notion of the loss of salvation by Jesus Christ raises profound questions about the nature of God's grace and the human ability to maintain a faithful relationship with Him. According to this, eternal life is conditional on the individual's ongoing faith and obedience. This stance highlights the importance of cultivating a personal relationship with The Lord, Jesus, God, regularly engaging in spiritual practices, and seeking forgiveness for wrongdoing. It also underscores the significance of human choice and the need for perseverance in the Christian journey.

In today's rapidly changing world, staying informed is crucial. Ignorance not only limits our ability to adapt and thrive but also puts us at a disadvantage compared to those who are knowledgeable. Without knowledge, we lack the skills and understanding necessary to navigate complex situations and make informed choices. This can result in missed opportunities, failed relationships, loss of salvation, and an overall diminished quality of life. It is essential to recognize the danger of ignorance and take steps to continually expand our knowledge base.

Furthermore, the danger of ignorance extends beyond individual lives. In a society where ignorance prevails, progress becomes stagnant, and division can arise. A lack of knowledge can lead to misunderstandings, prejudice, and intolerance, further fueling social and cultural conflicts. Collectively, it is our responsibility to promote education and awareness to counteract the dangers posed by ignorance. By encouraging learning and embracing knowledge, we can create a more informed and compassionate society that values growth and understanding.

In conclusion, the danger of ignorance is real and can have a significant impact on your life. By actively seeking out knowledge and information, you can avoid the pitfalls of ignorance and lead a more fulfilling and successful life. Ignorance is not simply a lack of information, but a barrier that prevents personal growth, critical thinking, and meaningful understanding of the world around us. When we remain uninformed, we limit our potential, make decisions based on incomplete or incorrect information, and become vulnerable to manipulation by others who may exploit our lack of knowledge.

Education is a powerful tool that breaks down these barriers, opening doors to new perspectives, opportunities, and personal development. By cultivating curiosity, embracing lifelong learning, and maintaining an open mind, individuals can continuously expand their understanding and adapt to an ever-changing world. Do not let ignorance hold you back - educate yourself and empower yourself to make informed choices. Seek out diverse sources of information, engage in meaningful conversations, challenge your own assumptions, and never stop learning.

Education is a powerful tool that breaks down these barriers, opening doors to new perspectives, opportunities, and personal development.

Remember that knowledge is not just about accumulating facts, but about developing the ability to think critically, make nuanced judgments, and navigate the complexities of modern life with confidence and wisdom.

Chapter 15

Discover the Truth about Salvation: A Spiritual Journey

13 In Him, you also, when you heard the word of truth, the good news of your salvation, and [as a result] believed in Him, were stamped with the seal of the promised Holy Spirit [the One promised by Christ] as owned and protected [by God].

(Ephesians 1:13) AMB

Salvation is a concept that holds great significance in many religious traditions around the world. It is often seen as the goal of a spiritual journey, the attainment of eternal peace and happiness. But what does salvation really mean, and how can one discover the truth about it through their own spiritual journey?

To begin with, salvation is commonly understood as the deliverance from sin and its consequences. In Christianity, for example, salvation is believed to come through faith in Jesus Christ and His sacrifice on the cross. Salvation can also be understood as a personal journey of self-discovery and transformation. It is about finding inner peace, purpose, and fulfillment in life. It is about letting go of negative emotions and beliefs that hold us back, and embracing love, compassion, and forgiveness.

Discovering the truth about salvation requires a willingness to explore our own beliefs and experiences, to question the teachings we have been given, and to seek out new perspectives. It involves a deepening of our spiritual practice, whether through prayer, meditation, or acts of service to others. It requires us to be open to the possibility of change and growth, to be willing to let go of old patterns and ways of thinking that no longer serve us.

Romans 12:2 (AMP)

And do not be conformed to this world [any longer with its superficial values and customs], but be transformed and progressively changed [as you mature spiritually] by the renewing of your mind [focusing on godly values and ethical attitudes], so that you may prove [for yourselves] what the will of God is, that which is good and acceptable and perfect [in His plan and purpose for you].

One way to embark on this spiritual journey of discovery is to engage in dialogue with others who have different beliefs and perspectives. By listening to their stories and sharing our own, we can gain new insights and deepen our understanding of the nature of salvation. We can also read books, attend workshops, and participate in spiritual retreats that challenge us to think differently and expand our horizons.

Ultimately, the truth about salvation is something that each of us must discover for ourselves. It is a deeply personal journey that requires courage, patience, and an open heart. It is a journey that may lead us to unexpected places, but one that promises great rewards in terms of inner peace, joy, and fulfillment.

So, if you are seeking to discover the truth about salvation, I encourage you to embark on your own spiritual journey. Be open to new ideas, be willing to question your beliefs, and be ready to embrace change.

Remember that salvation is not something that can be given to you by others; it is something that you must find within yourself. And as you travel along this path of self-discovery, may you find the peace and happiness that you seek.

In the search for meaning and purpose, many embark on a spiritual journey to discover the truth about salvation. This journey asks fundamental questions about existence, faith, and the ultimate destination of the soul. The truth about salvation lies in the belief that it is a transformative experience, a path towards redemption and Divine grace. People from all walks of life embark on this spiritual journey, seeking solace, enlightenment, and a connection with something greater than themselves. It is an exploration of one's innermost being, a quest to understand the mysteries of life and death.

The truth about salvation cannot be found in any external entity or institution; it resides within the depths of one's own awareness. This spiritual journey involves introspection, self-examination, and a willingness to confront one's fears and limitations. It requires a surrendering of ego, a letting go of attachments, and a sincere desire for self-improvement and spiritual growth. The path towards salvation is not one of blind adherence to dogma but rather a deeply personal experience that transcends religious boundaries. It is a quest to discover the universal truths that underpin human experience.

Embarking on a spiritual journey towards the truth about salvation is not a simple undertaking. It requires dedication, patience, and an open mind. Along this path, individuals may encounter moments of doubt, setbacks, and even moments of despair. Yet, it is through these trials that true growth and transformation occur. Through the challenges faced on this journey, individuals discover their own strength, resilience, and capacity for compassion. Ultimately, the truth about salvation is not a destination to be reached, but rather an ongoing process of self-discovery and spiritual evolution. It is a journey that lasts a lifetime, enriching one's existence and connecting them to something greater than themselves.

Ultimately, the truth about salvation is not a destination to be reached, but rather an ongoing process of self-discovery and spiritual evolution.

Chapter 16

The Importance of Saving Yourself: Learn Why You Should Act Now

12 So then, my dear ones, just as you have always obeyed [my instructions with enthusiasm], not only in my presence, but now much more in my absence, continue to work out your salvation [that is, cultivate it, bring it to full effect, actively pursue spiritual maturity] with awe-inspired fear and trembling [using serious caution and critical self-evaluation to avoid anything that might offend God or discredit the name of Christ].

(Philippians) 2:12 AMB

In today's fast-paced world, it is easy to get caught up in the hustle and bustle of everyday life. We often find ourselves putting others' needs before our own, neglecting our own well-being in the process. However, it is crucial to remember the importance of saving yourself and taking care of your own needs.

One of the main reasons why it is important to save yourself is that you cannot pour from an empty cup. If you are constantly giving to others without taking the time to replenish your own energy and resources, you will eventually burn out. This can lead to feelings of exhaustion, resentment, and even physical illness. By prioritizing self-care and saving yourself, you will be better equipped to help others and be a positive force in the world.

Another reason why saving yourself is important is that it allows you to live a more fulfilling and authentic life.

When you take the time to nurture your own needs and desires, you will be better able to pursue your passions and goals. This can lead to increased happiness, satisfaction, and overall well-being. By saving yourself, you are investing in your own future and creating a life that aligns with your values and aspirations.

So. Do not wait until you are completely burnt out or overwhelmed to prioritize self-care. Take small steps each day to nurture your mind, body, and spirit. This could include setting aside time for relaxation, exercise, hobbies, prayers, or spending time with loved ones and God. Remember, self-care isn't selfish – it is essential for your overall health and happiness.

Salvation is a concept that extends beyond the spiritual realm; it also encompasses actions taken to ensure our own well-being and personal. In today's fast-paced and demanding world, it is crucial to prioritize saving ourselves. By actively seeking personal salvation, we can safeguard our mental and physical health, cultivate resilience, and nurture a strong sense of self-worth. Saving yourself means recognizing the need for self-care, setting boundaries, and engaging in activities that promote personal development. It is an investment in your long-term happiness and overall satisfaction with life.

Personal salvation is not a luxury but a necessity. In a society where stress and burnout have become commonplace, saving yourself is an act of self-preservation. By proactively managing our physical and mental well-being, we can better handle life's challenges and bounce back from setbacks.

Moreover, saving ourselves allows us to make better choices and prioritize what truly matters to us. It empowers us to let go of toxic relationships, break free from harmful habits, and channel our energy into pursuits that align with our values and aspirations. Ultimately, acting now to save yourself is an investment in building a fulfilling and purpose-driven life.

The importance of saving yourself cannot be overstated, especially in a world that constantly demands more from us. Without taking steps to preserve our well-being, we risk falling into a cycle of exhaustion, stress, and dissatisfaction. By prioritizing self-care and personal development, we create a solid foundation for success in all areas of our lives. Saving yourself means recognizing that you are worthy of love, respect, and happiness. It involves setting healthy boundaries, nurturing positive relationships, and embracing personal growth opportunities. So, why wait? Act now to save yourself and unlock a future filled with abundance and fulfillment.

Saving yourself is of utmost importance as it encompasses the concept of personal salvation and true redemption. This notion has been prevalent in various religious and philosophical teachings, including Christianity. In Christianity, Jesus is the ultimate Savior, offering His life for the redemption of humanity. However, it is vital to understand that salvation goes beyond religious connotations and extends to personal growth and inner transformation.

The act of saving oneself entails taking responsibility for one's own life and actions. It involves acknowledging one's flaws and seeking ways to improve oneself. By recognizing the need to change and grow, individuals can embark on a journey towards personal salvation. This journey requires introspection, self-reflection, and a genuine desire for self-improvement. Ultimately, saving yourself means taking control of your life and steering it in a positive and fulfilling direction.

Furthermore, salvation and redemption are closely intertwined, as they both offer opportunities to overcome past mistakes and make amends. By saving yourself, you open the possibility of redemption and finding inner peace. It is a continuous process that requires dedication and perseverance. Through personal growth and transformation, individuals can learn from their past experiences, let go of regrets, and forge a path towards a brighter future.

In conclusion, the importance of saving yourself transcends spiritual beliefs and extends to personal development and growth. Taking responsibility for one's life, seeking self-improvement, and finding redemption are all part of this process. Whether through religious teachings like those found in Christianity or through self-reflection and inner transformation, saving yourself is a vital endeavor. It offers the possibility of personal salvation and true redemption, enabling individuals to lead a fulfilling and purposeful life. So, why wait? Act now and embark on the journey of saving yourself.

The journey of personal transformation is a profound and multifaceted odyssey that transcends simplistic boundaries of religious doctrine. Saving oneself is not a singular act of dramatic intervention, but a deeply introspective, compassionate, and intentional process of continuous self-discovery and growth. This transformative path interweaves elements of psychological resilience, emotional intelligence, spiritual awareness, and personal accountability, creating a rich tapestry of human potential and renewal.

Christianity offers powerful narratives of redemption and inner healing; the essence of personal salvation extends far beyond theological constructs. It encompasses a holistic approach to self-understanding—recognizing one's inherent worth, confronting internal limitations, healing past wounds, and consciously choosing personal evolution. This journey demands courage, vulnerability, and an unwavering commitment to self-reflection.

The process of saving oneself is not about achieving a perfect, unchanging state, but about embracing the dynamic nature of human experience. It involves cultivating self-compassion, developing emotional agility, and understanding that personal growth is a nonlinear progression marked by moments of insight, challenge, setback, and profound transformation. Each individual's path is unique, shaped by personal experiences, cultural context, psychological makeup, and intrinsic motivations.

True personal redemption emerges not from external prescriptions or quick fixes, but from a deep, sustained engagement with The Lord, and one's inner landscape. It requires dismantling limiting beliefs, challenging ingrained behavioral patterns, and courageously reimagining one's narrative. This process is simultaneously an act of deconstruction and reconstruction—letting go of what no longer serves while carefully, intentionally building a more authentic, empowered sense of self.

By embracing this comprehensive approach to personal transformation, individuals can unlock remarkable potential for healing, growth, and meaningful living. The journey of saving oneself becomes less about dramatic rescue and more about mindful, compassionate self-creation—a lifelong commitment to becoming the most authentic, resilient, and actualized version of oneself.

Part Number Five
Scene Five: The Message of the Cross

Chapter 17

From the Beginning: Uncovering the Secrets of Our Existence

9 and to make plain [to everyone] the plan of the mystery [regarding the uniting of believing Jews and Gentiles into one body] which [until now] was kept hidden through the ages in [the mind of] God who created all things.

(Ephesians 3:9) AMB

The Purpose of Creation. God had specific reasons for the creation of the world.

(1) God created the Heavens and the Earth as a manifestation of His glory, power, and majesty. David says, "The Heavens declare the glory of God, and the firmament declares the work of His hands" (Psalms 19:1; cf. Psalms 8:1). By contemplating the entire created cosmos – from the immense space of the universe created to the beauty and order of nature -, one cannot help but admire the majesty of the Lord God, the Creator.

(2) God created the Heavens and the Earth to receive the glory, and honor due to Him. All the elements of nature – e.g., the sun and the moon, the trees of the forest, the rain and snow, the rivers and streams, the hills

and mountains, the animals and birds – give voices of praise to the God who He did (Psalms 98:7-8; 148:1-10; Isaiah 55:12).

How much more does God desire and expect to receive glory and praise from human beings!

(3) God created the earth to provide a place where His purpose and purposes for mankind could be fulfilled.

(a) God created Adam and Eve in His own image so that He could have a loving, personal relationship for all eternity. God conceived the human being as a triune being (body, soul, spirit) who possesses mind, emotion, and will so that he can respond spontaneously to Him as Lord, and worship and serve Him with faith, fidelity, and gratitude.

(b) God so desired that intimate relationship with the human's race that, when Satan succeeded in tempting Adam and Eve to rebel and disobey God's commandment, He promised to send a Savior to redeem the human's race from the consequences. Of sin (see Genesis 3:15, note). In that way, God would have a people for Himself who would enjoy Him, glorify Him, and live in righteousness and Holiness before Him (Isaiah 60:21; 61:1-3; Ephesians 1:11-12; 1 Peter 2:9).

(c) The culmination of God's purpose in creation is recorded in the Book of Revelation, where John describes the end of history with these words: "And he will dwell with them, and they will be His people, and God himself will be with them." Them as their God" (Revelations 21:3).

Chapter 18

After the Beginning: A Story About Starting Something New

20 For if, after they have escaped the pollution of the world by [personal] knowledge of our Lord and Savior Jesus Christ, they are again entangled in them and are overcome, their last condition has become worse for them than the first.

(2 Peter 2:20) AMB

After the beginning, there is always something new waiting to unfold. It is like turning the page of a book and discovering a whole new chapter, filled with excitement and possibilities. This is the essence of life - a continuous journey of beginnings and endings, each leading to something fresh and unknown.

In the story of our lives, every new beginning is like a blank canvas, waiting to be painted with our hopes, dreams, and aspirations. It is a chance to start afresh, to leave behind the past, and embrace the future with open arms. Whether it is starting a new job, moving to a new city, or embarking on a new relationship, each new beginning brings with it a sense of anticipation and excitement.

Keywords such as growth, change, and opportunity come to mind when we think of new beginnings. These are the building blocks of a fulfilling and meaningful life, where we are constantly evolving and adapting to the ever-changing world around us. It is through these new beginnings that we discover our true potential and learn to navigate the challenges that come our way.

The tone of a new beginning is often relaxed, as we let go of the pressures and expectations of the past and allow ourselves to simply be in the present moment. It is a time to reflect on where we have been and where we want to go, without the constraints of judgment or fear. It is a time to be gentle with ourselves, to trust in the process of growth and change, and to embrace the unknown with a sense of curiosity and wonder.

So, as we embark on new beginnings in our lives, let us remember to stay relaxed and open to the possibilities that lie ahead. Let us trust in our own resilience and strength and have faith that each new beginning is a step towards a brighter and more fulfilling future. Embrace the unknown with a sense of calm and confidence, knowing that every new beginning is a chance to create something beautiful and meaningful.

After the beginning, when the world was still young and full of possibilities, a remarkable story unfolded. It is the story of Jesus Christ, a Divine God, who came to Earth to bring Light and hope to humanity. With His teachings of love and redemption, Jesus became a symbol of new beginnings, offering solace to those seeking guidance in a troubled world. However, His mission was not without opposition. Satan, a formidable force of darkness, sought to thwart Jesus' efforts at every turn.

But despite the challenges he faced, Jesus remained steadfast, drawing strength from the celestial realms and the support of angels like Michael, who tirelessly fought alongside Him to ensure that His message resonated with all who sought salvation.

After the beginning, the story of Jesus Christ unfolded like a deeply moving narrative, punctuated by moments of profound significance. From His humble birth in Bethlehem to His miracles and teachings, Jesus was a catalyst for change, a beacon of hope in a world fraught with despair.

But within this tale of inspiration, there existed a stark contrast in the form of Satan, the embodiment of evil and temptation.

As Jesus walked the Earth, Satan sought to exploit His vulnerabilities, tempting Him with power, wealth, and the allure of a more expedient path. However, Jesus resisted, staying true to His purpose, His unwavering resolve bolstered by the unwavering support of the angel Michael.

After the beginning, the story of Jesus Christ and His encounter with Satan unfolded with a poignant complexity that transcended the mere physical realm, revealing a profound spiritual confrontation that would ultimately define the trajectory of human salvation. It was a battle between Light and darkness, virtue and corruption, and ultimately, a testament to the enduring strength of the human spirit and Divine purpose.

In the face of opposition that seemed insurmountable, Jesus exemplified an unwavering faith and determination that went far beyond human capability, drawing upon a celestial wisdom that challenged the very foundations of spiritual warfare. The temptation in the wilderness became more than a singular moment of trial; it was a pivotal narrative that demonstrated the profound spiritual resilience inherent in Divine love and purpose.

Michael, the celestial warrior, stood as a powerful symbol of protection and support, representing the Divine ecosystem of spiritual defense that surrounds those who remain steadfast in their faith. His presence was not merely symbolic but a manifestation of Heavenly intervention, ensuring that Jesus was equipped with the spiritual tools and inner strength to combat the relentless and insidious influence of Satan. This encounter was a microcosm of the larger spiritual struggle between good and evil, revealing the intricate dynamics of temptation, resistance, and ultimate triumph.

The narrative went beyond a simple confrontation, instead presenting a nuanced exploration of spiritual sovereignty, free will, and the transformative power of unwavering belief. Together, Jesus and the

Divine forces defied the odds, creating a moment that would reverberate through centuries of human experience, leaving an indelible mark on humanity's collective consciousness. This story became more than a historical or religious account; it transformed into a universal narrative of hope, inspiring generations to find solace, strength, and new beginnings in the face of seemingly insurmountable adversity, and offering a profound testament to the power of faith to overcome darkness.

Chapter 19

Understanding Satan's Plans: How to Avoid Falling into His Traps

The oracle of one who hears the words of God,
Who sees the vision of the Almighty,
Falling down, but having his eyes open and uncovered,

(Numbers 24:4) AMB

Satan, also known as the Devil, is often portrayed as a sinister figure who is constantly trying to lead people astray and tempt them into sin. While this may be true to some extent, it is important to understand that Satan's plans are not always obvious and can be much more subtle than we realize. To avoid falling into his traps, it is crucial to have a clear understanding of his tactics and how to resist them.

One of Satan's main strategies is to deceive and manipulate people into believing lies about themselves, others, and even God. He often preys on our insecurities, fears, and desires, leading us to make choices that are harmful to ourselves and others. By recognizing these lies and replacing them with the truth of God's word, we can protect ourselves from falling into Satan's traps.

Another common tactic of Satan is to tempt us with worldly pleasures and distractions that lead us away from God. Whether it be material possessions, power, or fame, Satan knows our weaknesses and will use them to try and lure us away from our faith. By staying grounded in our relationship with The Lord, Jesus, God, and focusing on what truly matters, we can resist these temptations and avoid falling into Satan's traps.

It is also important to remember that Satan is a master of manipulation and will stop at nothing to try and destroy our faith. He may use other people, circumstances, or even our own thoughts to try and lead us astray. By staying vigilant and seeking guidance from God through prayer and scripture, we can protect ourselves from falling into Satan's traps.

To effectively avoid falling into Satan's traps, it is crucial to gain a deep understanding of his plans and strategies. Satan, also known as The Devil, is believed to be an adversary of both The Lord, Jesus, God, and humanity in various spiritual and cultural traditions. His goal is to lead individuals astray from righteousness and encourage them to engage in sinful and harmful actions. By studying and comprehending Satan's plans, we can equip ourselves with the necessary knowledge to resist his temptations and remain steadfast in our faith.

Satan's plans primarily revolve around exploiting our weaknesses and vulnerabilities. He is aware of our tendencies and inclinations towards sinful behavior, and he cunningly uses this knowledge to ensnare us into his traps.

These traps can manifest in various forms, such as temptations, doubts, or distractions, and they are designed to provoke us to deviate from the path of righteousness. It is important to recognize that no one is immune to these traps, and we must be vigilant and proactive to safeguard ourselves against them.

To avoid falling into Satan's traps, it is crucial to strengthen our spiritual resolve and fortify our faith. This can be achieved through regular prayer, meditation, studying sacred texts, and surrounding ourselves with a strong support system of like-minded individuals. Furthermore, it is important to cultivate self-awareness and introspection, as this enables us to identify and address our own weaknesses and areas of vulnerability. By turning to God for guidance, seeking His protection, and relying on His strength, we can effectively steer clear of Satan's plans and remain on the righteous path.

In conclusion, understanding Satan's plans and tactics is crucial to navigating the spiritual battlefield that exists beyond our physical perception. The enemy's strategies are complex and multifaceted, designed to exploit our vulnerabilities, undermine our faith, and create distance between us and God's Divine purpose.

By recognizing his lies—which often masquerade as seemingly rational thoughts, subtle doubts, or attractive but destructive temptations—we develop a spiritual discernment that acts as our most powerful defense. These lies frequently target our deepest insecurities, past wounds, and unresolved emotional struggles, attempting to manipulate our perception and lead us away from our true spiritual identity. Resisting his temptations requires more than willpower; it demands a comprehensive approach of spiritual discipline, constant prayer, biblical understanding, and genuine community support.

Staying grounded in our faith means cultivating a deep, intimate relationship with The Lord, Jesus, God that becomes our primary source of strength, wisdom, and protection. This relationship transforms us from being merely reactive to Satan's schemes to becoming proactively aligned with God's transformative power.

Satan may employ psychological warfare, using fear, shame, guilt, and confusion as his primary weapons, but these tactics lose their power when we understand our true identity as beloved children of God. Remember, Satan may be powerful in the temporal realm, but he is ultimately a defeated enemy whose power is limited and temporary. With God on our side, we are not just survivors, but more than conquerors—equipped with spiritual armor, Divine wisdom, and an unbreakable connection to the ultimate source of power and love. Stay strong in your convictions, remain faithful through both trials and triumphs, and trust completely in God's perfect plan for your life, knowing that His love and protection far surpass any scheme the enemy might devise.

> With God on our side, we are not just survivors, but more than conquerors—equipped with spiritual armor, Divine wisdom, and an unbreakable connection to the ultimate source of power and love

Part Number Six
Scene Six: The Power of Forgiveness: Why Letting go is Key to Healing

Chapter 20

The Power of Soul Healing: Transform your Life with Spiritual Cleansing

To cleanse the house then, he shall take two birds and cedar wood and scarlet string and hyssop;

Leviticus 14:49 (AMB)

In today's fast-paced world, it's easy to get caught up in the hustle and bustle of everyday life. We often find ourselves overwhelmed with stress, anxiety, and negative emotions that can weigh us down and prevent us from living our best lives. But what if there was a way to cleanse our souls and transform our lives for the better?

Spiritual cleansing is a powerful practice that has been used for centuries to help individuals release negative energy, heal emotional wounds, and restore balance to their lives. By connecting with our inner selves and The Lord, Jesus, God that surrounds us, we can tap into a source of healing and transformation that can bring about profound changes in our lives.

One of the key benefits of spiritual cleansing is its ability to help us let go of past traumas and negative experiences that may be holding us back. By releasing these emotional burdens, we can create space for new opportunities, growth, and abundance to enter our lives. This process can help us break free from old patterns and beliefs that no longer serve us, allowing us to move forward with a renewed sense of purpose and clarity.

In addition to healing emotional wounds, spiritual cleansing can also help us cultivate a deeper sense of connection with ourselves and the world around us. By tuning into our inner wisdom and intuition, we can gain valuable insights and guidance that can help us navigate life's challenges with grace and ease. This sense of connection can also help us feel more grounded, centered, and at peace, even during chaos and uncertainty.

The power of soul healing lies in its ability to transform our lives from the inside out. By clearing away negative energy and aligning ourselves with The Lord, God, we can create a life that is filled with joy, abundance, and fulfillment. This transformation can help us attract positive experiences and relationships, manifest our deepest desires, and live in alignment with our true purpose and potential.

To experience the transformative power of soul healing, it's important to approach the practice with an open heart and mind. Set aside time each day for quiet reflection, meditation, and prayer to connect with your inner self and The Lord, Jesus, God that surrounds you. Trust in the process and allow yourself to release any resistance or fear that may be holding you back.

Spiritual cleansing is a practice that has the power to bring about a transformation in your life. It is a process that involves purifying your spirit and releasing negative energies that may hinder your personal growth. Through spiritual healing, you can restore balance and harmony to your mind, body, and soul. By addressing the root cause of any emotional or physical imbalances, you can experience a profound shift in your well-being. Spiritual cleansing offers a holistic approach to self-care, to unlock your potential and create a life of joy and fulfillment.

Embarking on a journey of spiritual healing through cleansing can have a profound impact on your life. It allows you to let go of old patterns, traumas, and negative energies that may be holding you back. By focusing on the purification of your soul, you can release emotional burdens and experience a renewed sense of clarity and purpose. Spiritual cleansing not only uplifts your spirit but also strengthens your connection with Divine power. Through this transformative practice, you can cultivate greater self-awareness, tap into your inner wisdom, and awaken the dormant potential within you.

The power of soul healing through spiritual cleansing lies in its ability to bring about a comprehensive transformation in your life. It goes beyond addressing superficial issues and delves deep into the core of your being. By clearing away energetic blockages and aligning your mind, body, and spirit, you can experience a profound shift in your overall well-being. Spiritual cleansing empowers you to let go of toxic emotions, thoughts, and behaviors, freeing yourself from the shackles of the past. It opens new avenues for growth, self-discovery, and spiritual evolution, enabling you to embrace a life of true authenticity and purpose.

As you embark on your soul-healing journey, remember to be gentle and patient with yourself. Healing is a process that takes time, so be kind to yourself as you navigate the ups and downs of your spiritual cleansing journey. Trust that God has a plan for you and that you are supported every step of the way.

Spiritual Cleansing through Jesus Christ

Part 1:

Spiritual cleansing through Jesus Christ is a profound practice that holds deep significance for many believers. This process involves seeking purification and renewal of the spirit through the intervention and guidance of Jesus Christ. Jesus, serves as a spiritual mediator, offering believers an opportunity to restore their connection with God and find inner peace. By surrendering to Jesus Christ and seeking spiritual cleansing, individuals hope to rid themselves of impurities and find spiritual restoration.

Part 2:

The concept of spiritual cleansing by Jesus Christ is rooted in the fact that humanity is inherently flawed and separated from God due to sin. However, through His sacrificial death and resurrection, Jesus offers a path to redemption and spiritual restoration. Believers understand that Jesus, as the Son of God, possesses the power to wash away their sins and purify their souls. By embracing Jesus as their spiritual guide and accepting His forgiveness, individuals can experience a profound transformation and find solace in knowing that they have been spiritually cleansed.

Part 3:

The process of spiritual cleansing by Jesus Christ holds great significance for individuals seeking salvation and spiritual renewal. By surrendering to Jesus and acknowledging Him as their savior, believers experience a spiritual rebirth and find solace in God's unending grace and love. Jesus' teachings and examples serve as a guiding light, helping individuals navigate the challenges of life and make wise choices that align with their renewed spiritual identity. The act of seeking spiritual cleansing and restoration through Jesus Christ provides believers with a sense of hope, purpose, and deep spiritual fulfillment.

In conclusion, spiritual cleansing is a powerful and transformative practice that invites us to journey deeper into our inner landscape, transcending the surface-level challenges of daily life to touch the profound depths of our spiritual essence; it is a deliberate and intentional path of self-discovery, healing, and spiritual renewal that requires courage, vulnerability, and an open heart.

By consciously releasing negative energy—those accumulated emotional residues, past hurts, and limiting beliefs that weigh down our spirit—we create space for Divine grace to enter and reconstruct our inner world. The act of healing emotional wounds becomes a holistic experience that integrates body, mind, and spirit, recognizing that true healing is not about erasing our past, but about understanding, accepting, and ultimately transforming our experiences into sources of wisdom and strength.

Connecting with our inner selves means learning to listen to the subtle whispers of our soul, to honor our intuition, and to recognize the Divine spark that resides within us. This connection allows us to align with a higher purpose, to understand our unique spiritual blueprint, and to navigate life's challenges with grace and resilience.

Spiritual cleansing is an ongoing journey of surrender, where we learn to trust in a power greater than ourselves—a Divine intelligence that guides, supports, and ultimately leads us toward our highest potential. So, take the time to nurture your soul with intention and love, creating sacred moments of reflection, prayer, and meditation. Relax into the knowledge that you are supported by a universal power that knows your deepest needs, and trust in the power of The Holy Spirit, God, and soul healing, to gently guide you on your path to a more fulfilling, purposeful, and spiritually aligned life.

Chapter 21

Fear and Self-Knowledge: How to Understand your Emotions and Over your Fears

'Do not fear [anything], for I am with you; Do not be afraid, for I am your God. I will strengthen you, be assured I will help you; I will certainly take hold of you with My righteous right hand [a hand of justice, of power, of victory, of salvation].'

[Acts 18:10] AMB

Fear is a powerful emotion that can often hold us back from reaching our full potential. It can manifest itself in many ways, from a fear of failure to a fear of the unknown. However, understanding our fears and learning how to overcome them is essential for personal growth and self-discovery.

Self-knowledge is the key to understanding our fears. By taking the time to reflect on our thoughts and emotions, we can begin to uncover the root causes of our fears. This self-awareness allows us to identify patterns in our behavior and thought processes, which can help us better understand why we feel the way we do.

One way to gain self-knowledge is through prayer, mindfulness practices, such as meditation or journaling. These activities can help us tune into our emotions, and thoughts, allowing us to better understand the underlying reasons for our fears. By becoming more aware of our fears, we can begin to address them head-on and work towards overcoming them.

It's important to remember that fear is a natural and normal emotion. It's okay to feel afraid, but it's also important not to let fear control us. By acknowledging our fears and working to understand them, we can begin to take steps towards overcoming them.

One way to overcome fear is to face the big giant. This may involve stepping outside of our comfort zone and confronting the things that scare us. By gradually exposing ourselves to our fears, we can begin to desensitize ourselves to them and build up our confidence in the process.

Another way to overcome fear is to practice self-compassion. It's important to be kind to ourselves and recognize that it's okay to feel afraid. By treating ourselves with love and understanding, we can begin to break free from the grip of fear and move towards a place of self-acceptance and empowerment.

Fear and self-knowledge are deeply intertwined aspects of human psychology. Understanding your emotions and overcoming your fears requires an introspective journey into the essence of who you are. Fear, as an emotion, often arises from a lack of self-knowledge. By delving deep within us and uncovering the root causes of our fears, we can begin to understand and dissolve them.

Self-knowledge allows us to explore the layers of our consciousness and gain a deeper understanding of our emotions. It is only through this self-exploration that we can truly comprehend the fears that hold us back. By understanding the triggers and underlying beliefs associated with our fears, we become empowered to overcome them. Self-knowledge also helps us identify patterns in our emotional responses, enabling us to develop healthier coping mechanisms.

To understand our emotions and overcome fears, it is essential to cultivate mindfulness and emotional intelligence. By being present in the moment and observing our emotions without judgment, we can better understand their origin and significance. This practice allows us to develop a deeper sense of self-awareness. Over time, we can train ourselves to respond to fear in a more mindful and rational manner, rather than being controlled by it.

Understanding Emotions and Fear:

1. The Nature of Fear

- Fear is a fundamental human emotion designed for survival
- It's an evolutionary mechanism that alerts us to potential threats
- Not all fears are rational or helpful in modern contexts

2. Types of Fear

- Survival fears (immediate physical danger)
- Psychological fears (rejection, failure, uncertainty)
- Learned fears (conditioned responses from past experiences)
- Existential fears (mortality, meaninglessness)

Self-Knowledge Process

1. Emotional Awareness

- Practice mindfulness and emotional observation
- Learn to sit with your emotions without judgment
- Develop a vocabulary to precisely describe your emotional states
- Recognize emotional patterns and triggers

2. Root Cause Analysis

- Trace fears to their original sources
- Examine childhood experiences
- Understand how past traumas shape current emotional responses
- Identify limiting beliefs that fuel your fears

3. Cognitive Reframing Techniques

- Challenge irrational fear-based thoughts
- Replace catastrophic thinking with realistic assessments
- Develop alternative narratives about your capabilities
- Use positive, empowering self-talk

Practical Strategies for Overcoming Fears

1. Gradual Exposure

- Create a hierarchy of fears
- Systematically confront fears in controlled, incremental steps
- Build emotional resilience through progressive challenges
- Celebrate small victories in facing your fears

2. Emotional Regulation Skills

- Learn deep breathing techniques
- Practice meditation and mindfulness
- Prayer- Connecting with the Lord
- Develop grounding strategies during intense emotional states
- Use visualization and positive imagery

3. Self-Compassion Approach

- Treat yourself with kindness during fearful moments
- Recognize that fear is a universal human experience
- Avoid self-criticism
- Develop a nurturing inner dialogue

4. Personal Growth Framework

- View fears as opportunities for transformation

- Understand that growth happens outside comfort zones
- Cultivate curiosity about your emotional landscape
- Adopt a learner's mindset

5. Professional Support

- Consider therapy or counseling
- Join support groups
- Work with coaches specializing in emotional intelligence
- Learn from others' experiences in managing fears

Additional Psychological Tools

1. Journaling

- Document your emotional journey
- Analyze fear patterns
- Track personal growth and insights
- Create a reflective practice

2. Physiological Awareness

- Understand mind-body connection
- Recognize physical manifestations of fear
- Develop holistic emotional health

Transformative Perspective

- Fear is not your enemy, but a messenger
- Each fear confronted is an opportunity for personal expansion
- Emotional intelligence is a learned skill
- Self-knowledge is a lifelong journey of discovery and healing

Recommended Practice:

1. Daily Emotional Check-in

- Spend 10-15 minutes in quiet reflection

- Ask yourself: What am I feeling? Why am I feeling this?

____

- Practice non-judgmental observation

- Note patterns and insights

2. Fear Deconstruction Exercise

- When experiencing fear, pause

- Ask: Is this fear rational?

____

- What's the worst possible outcome?

____

- What resources do I have to address this situation?

____

In conclusion, fear and self-knowledge are interconnected in profound ways. Understanding our emotions and delving into the depths of our consciousness is the key to overcoming our fears. By embarking on this journey of self-discovery, we gain valuable insights into ourselves, develop healthier coping strategies, and ultimately find the path to personal growth and freedom from fear.

Fear is a natural emotion that everyone experiences at some point in their lives. By gaining self-knowledge and understanding our fears, we can begin to take steps towards overcoming them. Through mindfulness practices, facing our fears head-on, and practicing self-compassion, we can learn to navigate our fears and move towards a place of personal growth and self-discovery. Remember, it's okay to feel afraid, but it's also important to take steps towards overcoming our fears and living a life free from their limitations.

Understanding and overcoming fears is not about elimination, but transformation. By developing self-knowledge, practicing emotional awareness, and adopting a compassionate approach, you can turn fear from a restrictive force into a catalyst for personal growth and empowerment.

Remember: Courage is not the absence of fear, but the decision that something else is more important than the fear.

Remember:

Courage is not the absence of fear, but the decision that something else is more important than the fear.

Chapter 22

Emotional Scarring: Discover the Power of Healing Your Inner Self

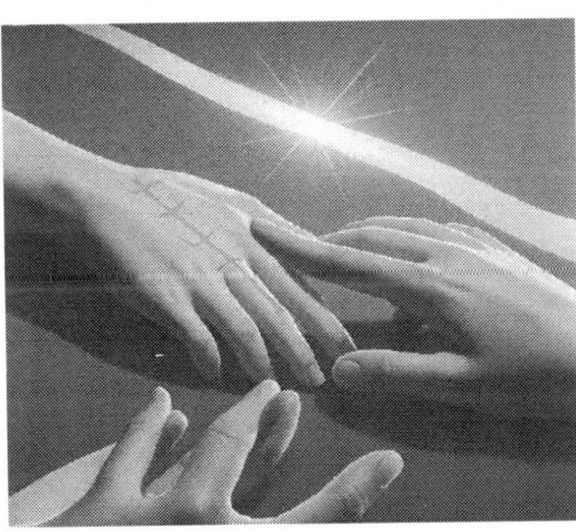

And one will say to him, 'What are these wounds between your arms?' Then he will answer, 'Those wounds I received in the house of my friends.'

Zechariah 13:6 (AMP)

Emotional scars are wounds that are not visible to the naked eye, but they can run deep and have a lasting impact on our mental and emotional well-being. These scars are often the result of past traumas, negative experiences, or unresolved emotions that have not been properly processed or healed. Just like physical scars, emotional scars can cause pain, discomfort, and hinder our ability to live a fulfilling life.

However, it is important to remember that emotional scars can be healed. Just as our bodies can heal physical wounds, our minds, and hearts also have the power to heal emotional wounds. The key to healing emotional scars lies in understanding and addressing the root causes of our pain and taking the necessary steps to heal and move forward.

One of the most powerful tools for healing emotional scars is self-reflection. By taking the time to explore our thoughts, feelings, and past experiences, we can gain a deeper understanding of the sources of our emotional pain and begin the process of healing. This can be done through journaling, therapy, prayer- connecting with the Lord, meditation, or simply taking the time to sit quietly and reflect on our emotions.

Another important aspect of healing emotional scars is self-compassion. It is important to be gentle and kind to us as we navigate the healing process. We must learn to forgive ourselves for past mistakes, let go of self-blame, and practice self-love and acceptance. By treating ourselves with compassion and understanding, we can begin to heal the wounds that have been holding us back.

In addition to self-reflection and self-compassion, seeking support from others can also be instrumental in healing emotional scars. Whether it is through therapy, support groups, or talking to trusted friends and family members, sharing our pain and struggles with others can help us feel less alone and more supported in our healing journey.

Ultimately, healing emotional scars is a process that takes time, patience, and dedication. It is important to remember that healing is not a linear process, and that setbacks and challenges may arise along the way. However, by staying committed to our healing journey and practicing self-care and self-compassion, we can begin to heal our emotional scars and live a more fulfilling and joyful life.

In conclusion, emotional scars can be healed, though the journey of healing is as unique and complex as the individual experiencing it. These invisible wounds, often deeply rooted in past traumas, painful experiences, and unresolved emotional challenges, do not define us but instead offer opportunities for profound personal growth and transformation. By taking the time to explore our emotions with patience and courage, we create a safe internal landscape where healing can gradually take root.

Practicing self-compassion becomes a revolutionary act of self-love—a gentle approach that acknowledges our pain without judgment and recognizes our inherent worth beyond our past experiences. Seeking support from trusted friends, family, therapists, prayer- connecting with the Lord, or support groups allows us to understand that vulnerability is not weakness, but a powerful form of strength that connects us to our shared human experience. The healing process is not linear; it involves moments of progress and setbacks, of breakthrough and reflection, of deep sorrow and unexpected joy.

Each step forward, no matter how small, is a testament to our resilience and inner strength. Remember, you are not alone in your healing journey, and with dedication, self-love, and a commitment to personal growth, you can gradually transform your emotional scars from sources of pain into marks of survival, wisdom, and ultimately, profound personal empowerment. Your healing is not just about overcoming past wounds, but about creating a future defined by hope, authenticity, and emotional freedom.

Chapter 23

Discovering the Heart of Jesus: Embracing the Message of Hope

Moreover, I will give you a new heart and put a new spirit within you, and I will remove the heart of stone from your flesh and give you a heart of flesh.

Ezekiel 36:26 (AMP)

In a world filled with chaos and uncertainty, it can be easy to lose sight of what truly matters. But amidst the noise and distractions, there is a message of hope that has been passed down through generations - the message of Jesus Christ.

Discovering the heart of Jesus is about embracing this message of hope and allowing it to transform our lives. It is about finding peace during turmoil, love in the face of hate, and joy amid sorrow.

The heart of Jesus is one of compassion, forgiveness, and grace. It is a heart that is open to all, regardless of their past mistakes or shortcomings. It is a heart that seeks to heal the broken and comfort the weary.

As we journey through life, it is important to remember the message of hope that Jesus brings. It is a message that reminds us that we are never alone, that there is always a light at the end of the tunnel, and that love conquers all.

Embracing the heart of Jesus means living a life of faith, hope, and love. It means extending a hand of kindness to those in need, speaking words of encouragement to the discouraged, and showing love to all. In a world that can often feel dark and hopeless, the message of Jesus shines like a beacon of Light. It is a message that reminds us that no matter how difficult our circumstances may be, there is always hope.

So let us take a moment to pause, to reflect, and to embrace the heart of Jesus. Let us allow His message of hope to fill our hearts and guide our actions. And let us remember that no matter what challenges we may face, we are never alone, for Jesus is always with us, offering us His love and grace.

Discovering the heart of Jesus is a transformative journey that allows individuals to embrace a profound message of hope. At the core of Christianity lies the teachings of Jesus, and by exploring His heart, we can gain a deeper understanding of His message. Jesus embodies compassion, love, and forgiveness, offering solace and redemption to those who seek it. Through studying His words and actions, we can uncover the essence of His teachings and incorporate these values into our own lives, ultimately fostering a sense of hope and purpose.

The heart of Jesus is characterized by boundless love and unwavering compassion. Jesus consistently demonstrated genuine care for others, offering healing and support to those who were marginalized and oppressed during His time. By embracing the heart of Jesus, individuals can learn to approach others with empathy and understanding, transcending societal divisions and fostering unity. This message of hope calls upon us to extend love and compassion to all, spreading the transformative power of Jesus' heart throughout the world.

Embracing the heart of Jesus also means embracing forgiveness and redemption. Jesus exemplified these virtues throughout His life, offering forgiveness to those who had wronged Him and extending a path towards salvation. This message of hope encourages individuals to seek forgiveness for their own transgressions and to extend forgiveness to others. By letting go of resentment and embracing the heart of Jesus, we open ourselves up to a renewed sense of hope and healing, both personally and in our relationships with others. It is through the heart of Jesus that we find the strength to overcome adversity and pursue a life filled with hope, forgiveness, and purpose.

In conclusion, discovering the heart of Jesus is about embracing the transformative message of hope that he brings to humanity. His teachings transcend mere religious doctrine, offering a profound pathway to understanding compassion, forgiveness, and unconditional love. It is about living a life of faith, hope, and love, allowing His teachings to guide us through life's most challenging moments and inspire us to become better versions of ourselves. Jesus' message invites us to look beyond our own limitations, to care for those who are marginalized, and to approach the world with empathy and grace.

By opening ourselves to His wisdom, we learn to see the Divine potential in every person, to extend mercy where judgment might be easier, and to find strength in vulnerability. So, let us open our hearts to Jesus and allow His message of hope to transform our lives, not just as a spiritual practice, but as a revolutionary way of engaging with the world around us—a path that leads to personal healing, community restoration, and a deeper understanding of what it means to truly love and be loved.

Part Number Seven
Scene Seven: Let's Meditate

Chapter 24

The Path to Salvation: Embracing Faith, Forgiveness, and Redemption

It is good that one waits quietly for the salvation of the Lord.
Lamentations 3:26 (AMP)

The path to salvation involves embracing faith, forgiveness, and redemption. Faith serves as the foundation, guiding individuals towards spiritual enlightenment and a deeper connection with The Lord Jesus, God. By having faith in a benevolent creator, individuals can find solace, strength, and the motivation to transform their lives. This transformation is facilitated through forgiveness, which plays a crucial role in the process of salvation.

By forgiving oneself and others, individuals can release the burdens of resentment and guilt, allowing for personal growth and spiritual liberation. In essence, faith and forgiveness intertwine, leading individuals down the path to salvation.

Redemption is another key element on the path to salvation. It is the process of seeking forgiveness and atonement for past wrongdoings. By recognizing the need for redemption and making amends, individuals can escape the consequences of their actions and achieve spiritual reconciliation.

Redemption requires one to confront their mistakes, acknowledge the harm caused, and actively work towards making positive changes. It is a transformative journey that requires sincere remorse, self-reflection, and a commitment to personal growth. Ultimately, redemption paves the way for salvation by allowing individuals to break free from the shackles of their past and strive for a brighter, more virtuous future.

The path to salvation is not a linear journey but rather a lifelong pursuit that requires dedication, self-discipline, and unwavering faith. It is a path filled with challenges, setbacks, and moments of doubt. However, those who remain steadfast and committed to their spiritual growth with the Lord, will ultimately find salvation.

The path is unique to everyone, as their beliefs, experiences, and personal circumstances shape their understanding of salvation. It is a personal quest that necessitates continuous self-improvement, seeking guidance from spiritual teachings, and nurturing a relationship with Jesus, God. By walking this path with integrity and genuine devotion, individuals can find the enlightenment, peace, and ultimate salvation they seek.

In life, we all face challenges and obstacles that can lead us astray from our true path. However, by embracing faith, forgiveness, and redemption, we can find our way back to salvation. The path of salvation is a journey that requires us to have faith in something greater than ourselves. Whether it be a spiritual belief, or simply trusting in The Lord, Jesus, God, having faith can provide us with the strength and guidance we need to navigate through life's trials and tribulations.

Forgiveness is another crucial aspect of the path to salvation. Holding onto grudges and resentments only serves to weigh us down and prevent us from moving forward. By practicing forgiveness, we can release ourselves from the burden of anger and resentment, allowing us to heal and grow spiritually.

Redemption is the final step on the path to salvation. It is the process of making amends for past mistakes and wrongdoings and seeking forgiveness from those we have hurt.

Redemption requires humility, honesty, and a willingness to change for the better. By seeking redemption, we can find peace and closure and move forward on our journey towards salvation.

Embracing faith, forgiveness, and redemption is not always easy, but it is essential for finding true peace and fulfillment in life. By trusting in something greater than us, letting go of past hurts, and seeking redemption for our mistakes, we can find our way back to the path of salvation.

So, as you navigate through life's ups and downs, remember to keep the faith, practice forgiveness, and seek redemption. By doing so, you can find your way back to salvation and live a life filled with love, peace, and joy.

The Path that Leads to Salvation:

1. During our existence, we inevitably encounter trials and hindrances that can sometimes divert us from our authentic purpose. It is in these moments that turning to faith, the power to pardon, and the opportunity for redemption becomes imperative to rediscover our path to salvation.

2. Life presents us with challenges and obstacles that can occasionally steer us away from our intended direction. However, in these circumstances, it is crucial to rely on faith, the ability to forgive, and the prospect of redemption, as they guide us towards finding true peace and attaining salvation.

3. Amidst the journey of life, we are often confronted with difficulties and hurdles that can occasionally lead us astray from our desired path. Nevertheless, it is during these critical moments that faith, forgiveness, and the chance for redemption act as guiding beacons, helping us rediscover the path that leads to salvation.

4. Our existence is colored by the inevitable presence of challenges and barriers that can sometimes veer us away from our ultimate purpose. Nonetheless, during these pivotal times, it is essential to embrace faith,

forgiveness, and the opportunity for redemption as they pave the way for finding true peace and attaining salvation.

5. Within the realms of life, we encounter various trials and stumbling blocks that may occasionally deviate from our intended trajectory. Yet, it is during these defining moments that we must seek solace in faith, the power of forgiveness, and the prospect of redemption, for they guide us towards the path that leads to genuine peace and salvation.

In conclusion, the path to salvation demands faith, forgiveness, and redemption— a transformative journey that challenges us to look beyond our human frailties and embrace a higher spiritual calling. By embracing these profound principles, we rediscover our true path, breaking free from the chains of past mistakes and the weight of personal struggles. Salvation is not a destination but a continuous process of spiritual growth, self-reflection, and Divine grace. It requires us to confront our deepest vulnerabilities, to acknowledge our imperfections, and to trust in a power greater than ourselves.

Through faith, we find the courage to face life's challenges; through forgiveness, we release the burden of resentment and pain; and through redemption, we experience the profound healing that comes from spiritual renewal. This journey is both deeply personal and universally significant, connecting us to a broader human experience of hope and transformation. So, let us embrace faith with an open heart, practice forgiveness with compassion, and seek redemption with humility as we continue the journey towards salvation—a path that leads us not just to personal peace, but to a deeper understanding of our place in the grand tapestry of existence.

Chapter 25

The Soul: Introduction to the Concept of the Soul

28 Do not be afraid of those who kill the body but cannot kill the soul; but rather be afraid of Him who can destroy both soul and body in hell. (Matthew 10:28) AMB

What is the soul in the Bible?

The soul, as explained in the Bible, represents the essence of a person, encompassing their life force and existence between death and the final resurrection. This concept emphasizes the understanding that human beings consist of both a physical body and an immaterial soul. The question arises: what occurs during the intermediate state between death and the ultimate resurrection?

The soul, derived from the Latin term "anima" and the Greek word "psyche", - signifies an immaterial entity that defines one's individuality and humanity. It serves as the vital force that animates life. In this sense, soul is synonymous with words like "psyche" (human soul), "vital breath", - "self" (the self), "individual", - "person", - or "inhabitant", -

Theological studies teach about the soul as a Divine element within an individual that endures beyond the demise of the physical body.

What are the components of the soul?

The soul constitutes the conscious aspect of our being, comprising the intellect, will, and emotions. These three components collectively form our conscious understanding of self.

What is the concept of soul?

Scriptures describe the soul as the vital force and emotional and intellectual aspect of a person. Hence, it represents the individual's very essence, personality, and sense of self.

Why is the human soul important?

The human soul holds significant importance in our existence as it defines our connection with God and enables us to experience and reflect His love and character in this world. According to Biblical teachings, the Holy Spirit works within individuals, purifying and safeguarding their souls.

What is the difference between the body and the soul?

The soul is regarded as the most intimate and spiritual part of a person, as it encompasses thoughts, emotions, willpower, and free choice. Unlike the physical body, which is temporary and vulnerable to death, the soul is eternal and destined for either the presence or absence of God, depending on one's individual choices.

In the realm of human existence, there has been an age-old debate concerning the composition of our beings. Specifically, whether we possess two parts (body and soul/spirit) or three parts (body, soul, and spirit). The dialogue surrounding this question has been influenced by spiritual texts, particularly, Genesis 1:26–27, which elucidates that God created mankind as separate from all other living beings. It is clear from Scripture that human beings are designed to have a relationship with God, and as such, we are a harmonious blending of both material (physical) and immaterial (spiritual) elements.

The material aspect of our being is the physical body, which is tangible and temporary. On the other hand, immaterial qualities are intangible and endure beyond the lifespan of the physical body. These include the soul, spirit, intellect, will, conscience, mind, and emotions, among others. These components exist in a cohesive and interconnected manner.

The nature of the soul, spirit, emotions, conscience, will, and mind is a subject of ongoing discussion. Some contend that the soul and spirit are combined to form a unified entity, while others maintain that the soul and spirit are interchangeable terms referring to the same spiritual reality. Both perspectives find support in Scripture, as various verses use the words soul and spirit interchangeably.

Alternatively, some scholars argue that humans possess three distinct parts: body, soul, and spirit. They point to passages such as 1 Thessalonians 5:23 and Hebrews 4:12, which appear to differentiate between the spirit and the soul. However, it is important to approach this debate with caution, as erroneous teachings can arise from an incomplete understanding.

Some proponents of the trichotomic view have espoused the idea that God can bypass our intellect and communicate directly with our spirit, leading to irrational mysticism. Additionally, there have been instances where certain churches have used the trichotomic position to advocate for the possibility of Christians being demon-possessed. Such teachings lack biblical support, as there is no evidence that those indwelt by the Holy Spirit can simultaneously be possessed by demonic forces.

Ultimately, the conclusive determination between dichotomy and trichotomy may not be of utmost importance. However, we can all stand united in praising The Lord, Jesus, God, for fearfully and wonderfully creating us, as expressed in Psalm 139:14. The question of the soul's meaning and composition is one that continues to intrigue humankind.

Exploring the Soul: A Journey Within

The concept of the soul has been a topic of fascination and contemplation for centuries. Many different cultures have their own beliefs and interpretations of what the soul is and its significance in our lives. In this chapter, we will explore the idea of the soul in a relaxed and easy-to-understand manner, delving into its meaning and how it can impact our daily lives.

So, what is the Soul?

The soul is often described as the spiritual essence of a person, the part of us that is eternal and transcends our physical body. It is believed to be the source of our emotions, thoughts, and consciousness. While the soul is intangible and cannot be seen or touched, many people believe in its existence and importance in shaping who we are.

The Purpose of the Soul

Many spiritual traditions believe that the soul has a specific purpose or mission in this lifetime. Some believe that the soul is on a journey of growth and evolution, learning important lessons and gaining wisdom along the way. Others believe that the soul is here to fulfill a specific destiny or to contribute to the greater good of humanity.

Connecting with Your Soul

There are many ways to connect with your soul and tap into its wisdom and guidance. Meditation, prayer, and mindfulness practices can help you quiet your mind and listen to the whispers of your soul. Spending time in nature, engaging in creative activities, and practicing self-care can also help you nurture your soul and deepen your connection to it.

Nurturing Your Soul

Just as our physical bodies need nourishment and care, our souls also require attention and nurturing. Taking time for self-reflection, practicing gratitude, and surrounding yourself with positive influences can help you nourish your soul and keep it healthy and vibrant. Remember to listen to your intuition and follow your heart's desires, as these are often messages from your soul.

In conclusion, the soul is a mysterious and profound aspect of our being, guiding us on our journey through life and helping us navigate its challenges and joys. By exploring the soul with an open heart and mind, we can deepen our understanding of ourselves and the world around us. Remember to take time to nurture your soul and listen to its wisdom, for it holds the key to living a fulfilling and purposeful life.

More than just a metaphysical concept, the soul represents the essence of our inner self - a complex tapestry of emotions, experiences, intuitions, and spiritual connections that transcend the physical realm. It serves as an internal compass, whispering insights and illuminating paths when our rational mind becomes clouded by doubt or external pressures. By exploring the soul with an open heart and mind, we can deepen our understanding of ourselves and the world around us, uncovering layers of meaning that often remain hidden beneath the surface of daily existence.

This profound inner landscape is not static but dynamically evolves through our experiences, relationships, and personal growth. Each moment of reflection, each challenge overcome, and each moment of genuine connection adds texture and depth to our soul's journey. The soul carries the wisdom of our ancestors, the dreams of our future, and the raw authenticity of our present moment. It invites us to look beyond superficial appearances and connect with something greater than our immediate circumstances.

Remember to take time to nurture your soul and listen to its wisdom, for it holds the key to living a fulfilling and purposeful life. This nurturing can take many forms - through meditation, creative expression, time in nature, meaningful conversations, or moments of quiet introspection. By creating space for our soul to speak, we open ourselves to profound insights, healing, and transformation that can guide us toward a more authentic and meaningful existence.

Collection of Inspirational Words by Authoress Adriana Brunga

I would like to extend my sincere appreciation for your generous support in acquiring this exceptional book. I trust that its contents have provided immense benefit to you. A percentage of the sales will be donated to God, specifically to aid orphanages. If this book has resonated with you on a deep level, I kindly request that you share your thoughts with me. It is to offer comment, request prayer, or even commit your life to the Lord, please do not hesitate to reach out by sending a message to ***adriana.brunga@gmail.com*** If this book has transformed your perspective on God, your personal testimony or comments are highly welcomed. We would be delighted to feature your experiences as a genuine testament to the all-encompassing love of God on our website at ***authoressadrianabrunga.com***

May the Lord Bless you abundantly. With love to all. *AB*

About the Author

Adriana Brunga, a native of Envigado in Medellin - Colombia, ventured across the Atlantic to the United States three and a half decades ago. Over the years, she has experienced the joys and sorrows of motherhood, with her wonderful children and daughter, Sarah Pineda, an accomplished twenty-six-year-old, and her eldest son, Jose, and youngest son, Diego, who are sadly no longer with us. Additionally, she relishes the company of two adorable grandchildren. Nine years ago, she entered introital bliss with her loving and remarkable husband, Bruno Brunga, who resided in Albania, Europe. They now live in Chester, South Carolina.

Before embarking on her writing career, Adriana was an independent entrepreneur in her own right. In her early years, she pursued educational pursuits, earning degrees in business administration, accounting, and psychological studies. Around eleven years ago, she transformed herself into an inspiring author on spiritual healing and a captivating public speaker on matters of the spirit. When not engrossed in the art of writing, she indulges her passion for reading, finding solace and enlightenment within the pages. She firmly believes that writing not only acts as an outlet for self-expression but also grants her spiritual liberation within her very being.

About the Book

This literary work serves as an educational tool, illuminating the authentic existence of the one and only living God, Jesus Christ. Yet, amidst the prevailing confusion in the world, individuals often misconstrue religion with various Divine beings. Personally, I have had the profound experience of encountering the true living God, Jesus Christ, who has Immense power in my life. Formerly, I adhered to a different deity and beseeched other virgins and saints to no avail.

However, when I found myself at a desperate impasse, it was Jesus Christ, the sole living God, who manifested His incredible resurrection power to resurrect me from my deathbed in the hospital. Inspired by this transformative event, I penned the book, " My Journey in the Afterlife with Jesus Christ," to chronicle the astoundingly powerful and compassionate nature of Jesus Christ.

Rooted in my own truthful narrative, I am confident that readers will gain a comprehensive understanding of Jesus Christ, the genuine living God. Primarily, the book aims to restore the fractured relationship between humanity and the Divine. With utmost gratitude to the Lord, I aim to elucidate how Jesus Christ saved both my spiritual and physical existence. As the author, a spiritual healing, my foremost intention is to guide readers to wholly embrace this book and allow it to deeply resonate, facilitating the healing of spiritual afflictions endured and granting the spiritual liberation that one's inner self craves.

Summary of the Book My Journey in the Afterlife with Jesus Christ by Authoress Adriana Brunga.

Protagonists:

- Jesus Christ - Divine being (Holy Spirit)

- Adriana Brunga - Author

- Dr. Lehman – Physician

In this captivating book, readers will witness a gripping narrative that takes unexpected twists and keeps the story grounded in the present. The plot unfolds as Adriana, the author, recounts a life-altering encounter with Jesus Christ at a hospital. The clock struck 7 P.M., and the room plunged into darkness. As Adriana gazed at the ceiling, a figure approached. It was Jesus Christ Himself. This encounter marked a turning point in her life, redirecting every aspect of her existence.

Adriana's journey starts with a tragic accident that leads to spinal surgery, followed by a five-day coma. Set in a hospital room in Columbia, SC, in 2009, the story delves into her recovery process. It is during this vulnerable time that Jesus Christ intervenes, saving her from the clutches of darkness when she was teetering on the edge. Her plea to Jesus was answered, and He became her Savior.

As the story reaches its climactic conclusion, readers witness Jesus Christ resurrecting Adriana, endowing her with a newfound purpose and a Divine presence within. Today, Adriana shares her incredible story, filled with gratitude and an unwavering desire to spread her testimony. This book encapsulates her journey and the joy that comes from being able to share it with readers around the world.

Other Published Books by Authoress Adriana Brunga

Death Saved by Jesus Christ - First edition – 2021.

Book Guarantee

This text summarizes the content of a book called "My Journey in the Afterlife with Jesus Christ" The book provides engaging and enlightening accounts of life after death with Jesus Christ. The author's personal enhances the reader's understanding and connection with the matter. The book is available in multiple formats for wider accessibility. It encourages thought-provoking reflections and fosters a meaningful spiritual connection with Jesus and the afterlife.

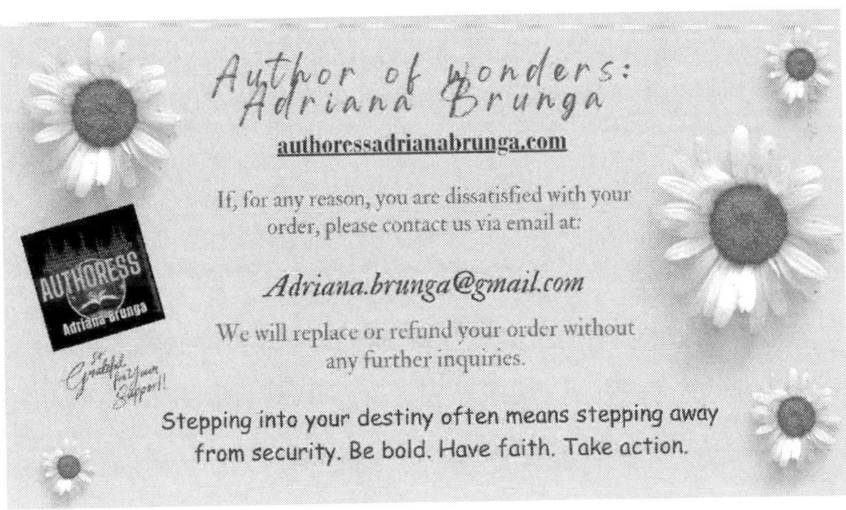

What is the Book About?

This book explores a wide range of captivating, delving into the depths of human emotions and spiritual healing. It goes beyond mere storytelling, challenging conventional beliefs offering readers a unique view on the world. Pages unravels profound insights, leaving a lasting impact on the reader's mind. Embark on a journey through the intricacies of human experience with this thought-provoking literary masterpiece.

Main topics:

The Difference Between Forgiveness and Reconciliation

Salvation

The Path of Salvation

God's Will

Repentance

The Difference Between Being Spiritual and Christian Spirituality

Death and Birth of the Soul (Spiritual Death)

The Power of Soul Healing

Introduction to the Concept of the Soul

Being Born Again

Being Saved

Believer

After the Beginning

Understanding Satan's Plans

How to Heal After the Loss: Grieving

Embracing and Accepting the Unexpected

Spiritual Healing

The Book Includes other themes such as:

Prayers

Meditation

Self-Reflection

Questions

And Message from Jesus

This book contains 25 chapters, 47,737 words, 272,602 characters and about 168+pages.

Made in the USA
Columbia, SC
27 April 2025